TEACHING TRUE LOVE TO A SEX-AT-13 GENERATION

The Ultimate Guide for Parents

ERIC AND LESLIE LUDY

W PUBLISHING GROUP™

www.wpublishinggroup.com

A Division of Thomas Nelson, Inc.
www.ThomasNelson.com

Published by W Publishing Group, a Division of Thomas Nelson, Inc., P. O. Box 141000, Nashville, Tennessee, 37214.

W Publishing Group books may be purchased in bulk for educational, business, fundraising, or sales promotional use. For information, please email SpecialMarkets@ThomasNelson.com.

All Scripture quotations, unless otherwise indicated, are taken from The Holy Bible, New International Version (NIV). Copyright © 1973, 1978, 1984. International Bible Society. Used by permission of Zondervan Bible Publishers.

Other Scripture references are from the following sources:

The King James Version of the Bible (KJV).

J. B. Phillips: The New Testament in Modern English, Revised Edition (PHILLIPS). Copyright © J. B. Phillips 1958, 1960, 1972. Used by permission of Macmillan Publishing Co., Inc.

New American Standard Bible (NASB). Copyright © 1960, 1962, 1964, 1968, 1971, 1973, 1975, 1977 by The Lockman Foundation, La Habra, California. Used by permission.

Cover Design: David Uttley, UDG/Design Works,
www. udgdesignworks.com

Published in association with Loyal Arts Literary Agency,
www.LoyalArts.com

Library of Congress Cataloging-in-Publication Data

Ludy, Eric.
 Teaching true love to a sex-at-thirteen generation / Eric & Leslie Ludy.
  p. cm.
Summary: "Guide for talking to teenagers today about abstaining from sex until marriage"—Provided by publisher.
Includes bibiographical references.

ISBN 0-8499-4256-X (tradepaper)

1. Chastity. 2. Christian teenagers—sexual behavior. 3. Child rearing—religious aspects—Christianity. 4. Sexual abstinence—Religious aspects—Christianity. 5. Sex instruction for teenagers—Religious aspects—Christianity. I. Ludy, Leslie. II. Title.

BV4647.C5L79   2005
241'.66—dc22   2005000912

Printed in the United States of America
05 06 07 08 RRD 9 8 7 6 5 4 3 2 1

Contents

Author's Note   ix

Unhappily Ever After   xv

PART ONE: A VISION FOR SOMETHING BETTER

Chapter 1:   3
Beyond Broken Promise Rings

Chapter 2:   21
Becoming a True-Love Teammate

PART TWO: A GOD-WRITTEN LOVE STORY

Chapter 3:   51
The Fuel of a God-Written Love Story

Chapter 4:   77
The Fire of a God-Written Love Story

PART THREE: PURITY THAT ENDURES

Chapter 5:   105
The Kind of Purity That Endures

Contents

Chapter 6:   129
The Catalyst for Purity That Endures

Part Four: True-Love Training

Chapter 7:   145
The Lasting Power of True-Love Training

Chapter 8:   163
The Lifelong Practice of True-Love Training

Part Five: Beyond Love Stories

Epilogue: 177
Shoulders of Giants

Bonus Section   189
Helping Kids Live Heroic Lives

Notes   215

God has so much more for our children than pop-culture conformity, spiritual atrophy, and sexual preoccupation. But for our kids to be among the rare few who push aside the mediocre life of selfishness and press forward into God's endless frontier, they need parents who are unwilling to let them settle in the land of compromise. Great parents, submitted to the vast potential of God, raise up great children.

Author's Note

Leslie

IT WAS JUST A SMALL PIECE of torn notebook paper. But the words it contained have haunted me for many years. In a child-like scrawl, a young girl had written a heart-wrenching message: "My mom is pressuring me to go out and date boys and have sex. I'm only twelve years old . . . help!"

Almost ten years have passed since I read that startling note. It was sent to me not long after Eric and I had begun working with young people around the country. I used to think that this young girl was merely an exception to the norm, that her mother was one of the few parents alive who was actually willing to taint her daughter's innocence in order to stay in step with the world's sexual program.

But after years of working with hundreds of thousands of youth and parents, Eric and I have come face to face with a disturbing reality. Today's sexual crisis hasn't merely crept into our pop culture . . . it has crept into our homes. The very place where kids should find a refuge from the slime of modern culture has often become the very place where their relational futures are undermined before they even begin.

If you have picked up this book, you are likely as concerned as we are for the future of today's younger generation. You've observed the disconcerting trends of modern youth, and you want something more for your children. You want to help them discover something better.

If that is how you feel, you are among a rare breed of parents today—parents willing to go the extra mile to help their kids escape today's sexual morass. And you are desperately needed. Because the rescue plan for today's sex-at-thirteen generation must start within our homes.

Over the past ten years, Eric and I have had the opportunity to interact closely with countless young people. They've shared their struggles, their fears, their desperation, and their dreams with us. They've given us a clear look into the battle they face on a daily basis—the intense pressure they feel to settle for the destructive cultural norm of our times. And over and over again, they've shared with us one of their deepest longings . . . a desire for heroic parents; parents who are willing to do whatever it takes to help them discover something better, parents who call them to a higher standard and offer them the support and practical guidance to help them reach it.

Recently I spent an intimate weekend with forty-eight Christian young women and heard their personal stories. Though most had Christian backgrounds, well over half of them had come from home environments plagued by sexual abuse, marital affairs, and/or divorce. A disturbingly high percentage of them had parents who never expected more for them than the typical path of sexual compromise. These young women had been left to face the pressure of the culture on their own. They were crying out for a support system, parents who would love them enough to point them toward something better. But typically, their parents were too absorbed with their own problems to notice how desperately their kids needed their guidance and godly example.

These young women are representative of an entire generation of young people that has been left to figure things out on their own. Today's parents are often so distracted by the downward spiral of their own lives that they fail to be the supporters and leaders the younger generation so acutely needs. As a result, today's young people all too often follow the deadly trends of the culture simply because no one has ever shown them a better way.

Our prayer is that this book will equip you, as a parent or leader, to become the answer to this generation's most urgent need. If the younger generation is ever to escape the slime of the culture and experience vibrant successful relationships and marriages, they need parents who will rise to the challenge and point them to God's highest.

We pray that this message will inspire you to embrace that sacred call.

This book is not written from a parent-to-parent perspective. Rather, this book is written from the *perspective of the younger generation*. We want this book to serve as a voice to you from today's young people. We want to help articulate their perspective and help you better understand what they need and desire from you as parents. We pray the words contained within these pages will give you a vision for your amazing role in the transformation of a generation, and offer you the practical tools to see that vision become a reality.

Eric and I were blessed with incredible parents—parents who, like you, were willing to go the extra mile to help their children discover something better than the cultural norm. Throughout this book, we give glimpses of our parents' personal journey and impact upon our lives. They have been gracious enough to allow us to openly share with you not only their victories, but their struggles and failures as well. It is not our parents' perfection, but their heart motivation that we seek to honor in this book. We are eternally grateful to them for the amazing foundation they have given us. We hope you will be inspired and uplifted by their example.

As you prepare to embark upon this journey, here are some things to keep in mind: First, throughout this book many names of people and places have been altered to protect privacy. Second, Eric and I have written many other books specifically geared for young people—to help them discover God's best in romance, relationships, and life. *When God Writes Your Love Story, When God Writes Your Life Story, When Dreams Come True, Authentic Beauty* (for girls) and *God's Gift to Women* (for guys) are powerful and practical books that solidify and deepen this message in a young person's life. We encourage you to use them as tools for passing a vision of godly romance along to your children. For more information, please visit our Web site: www.whengodwrites.com.

Eric and I have spent the past ten years fighting on behalf of today's younger generation. We have an unquenchable passion to see young people shake off modern mediocrity and discover the matchless wonder of a God-built future. We've seen incredible things happen on this journey; we've seen young lives forever changed through God's faithfulness. But the battle is far from over. And we can't fight this battle alone. We need you. As a parent, you are irreplaceable in grooming this generation for greatness.

So together, let's enter the fray. Let's seize the God-given opportunity we have to impact today's young people for eternity.

Unhappily Ever After

The heartbreaking story of today's sex-at-thirteen generation

Leslie

I WAS TEN YEARS OLD when I became the target of graphic sexual jokes on the playground.

I was eleven when I started being touched and grabbed sexually in the halls at school.

I was twelve when some of my peers began experimenting with oral sex and invited me to join in.

I was thirteen when I had my first opportunity to lose my virginity—to a fifteen-year-old boy I had known for two days.

I was fourteen when my friends began swapping sex stories at slumber parties—jovially comparing the size and stamina of their boyfriends' sexual organs.

And I was fifteen when I gave myself emotionally and physically to the first of several boys who used me for their own selfish pleasure and then mercilessly broke my heart.

No, I did not come from a broken home or rough neighborhood. I lived in a quiet suburb and was raised in a strong Christian household. I met most of my friends in Christian environments. My parents were loving, attentive, and supportive. They modeled a healthy marriage and taught me about purity from a young age.

So what went wrong? Why wasn't I sheltered from such intense sexual perversion in my early years? And with my solid Christian upbringing, why didn't I make better choices?

Was I just an oddity, an exception to the idea that kids with Christian backgrounds can usually avoid the kind of sexual pitfalls I succumbed to? Or is my story more common than many Christian parents realize?

The answer may startle you.

A GAME OF SURVIVAL

Things have changed quite dramatically in youth culture over the past few generations. When my mom was thirteen, she was still playing with Hula Hoops and Chatty Cathy dolls. By the time I was thirteen, I was being offered cigarettes and beer and receiving lewd propositions from greasy-haired fifteen-year-old guys. I lived in a world that I felt my parents could never understand. And like many teens, I worked hard to keep the reality of my world hidden from them.

I had always been exceptionally close to my mom and dad. When I was younger, I used to share everything with them. But that began to change after my first day of seventh grade. I will never forget walking down the halls of my junior high school that morning. In the span of five minutes, I was exposed to more filth, profanity, and perversion than the sum total of every R-rated movie and raunchy music video my parents had sheltered me from. Graphic sexual jokes, extreme and violent cursing, couples passionately groping each other, and a group of boys playing with an inflated condom were just a few of the sights and sounds that surrounded me in those moments. And that didn't include the drugs that were passed around in the back of my math class, the boy who kept his genitals exposed during an entire forty-five-minute history class, and the group of guys who took turns feeling up two girls on the bus ride home.

I didn't attend a gang-riddled school in a bad part of town. I lived in an upscale suburban neighborhood and went to a highly respected middle school that had a solid reputation. But that did not shelter me from the extreme pressure and perversion I faced on a moment-to-moment basis.

At the age of thirteen, I was thrust into a game of survival. Kids who did not conform to the crowd were mercilessly and systematically destroyed. It went far beyond the kind of "peer pressure" that well-meaning adults had tried to warn me about. It wasn't about "just saying no" to drugs, cigarettes, or sex. It wasn't about choosing the "right" group of friends. The filth and depravity seemed impossible to escape, no matter where I went or which friends I chose.

Anyone who attempted to stand for something different inevitably regretted that decision. They were mocked and ridiculed, and even physically attacked in some cases. A boy who had fallen into the bad graces of several popular guys was taken outside and urinated on. A girl who had gained a reputation as a prude was surrounded by a group of guys, her hands pinned behind her back as they lifted up her shirt in front of a classroom of students before the teacher arrived. These were punishments no thirteen-year-old could endure without severe emotional damage. I quickly decided that keeping my mouth shut wasn't a choice; it was a life necessity.

So I trained myself to survive each day, laughing at the perverted jokes and graphic propositions, giggling carelessly when I was touched sexually by guys I hardly knew, and becoming callous to the debauchery that swirled around me every day. I even began to join in the perversion, exchanging sexual banter with guys, flaunting my body with sensual clothes, and flirting shamelessly with anyone of the opposite sex. Inwardly, I was miserable. Though I held myself back from the major compromises, such as sex, drugs, alcohol, I knew that my words and actions defied everything I had once believed. But I saw no other way.

I resented my parents for being so out of touch with my world. They were loving and concerned, but naive. When they sat down with me to have "the talk" about sex, they said things like, "One day, when you start dating, a boy may try to put his hand on your knee. That's a sign that you need to stop him before things go any further." Little did they know that nearly every day I was engulfed in sexual pressure far beyond anything they could imagine. I didn't know how to tell them. I thought that they would somehow blame me. I pictured them giving me useless advice, such as "You just need to stand up for what you believe!"

At thirteen, I didn't even know how to articulate the intensity of the world I lived in. It took all of my energy and emotional strength just to make it through each day without losing my sanity. I didn't know how to cry out for help. And I didn't believe my parents could help me, even if they tried.

So for the next several years, I put up a wall of deception between my parents and myself. I knew what they needed to hear in order not to worry. As long as they thought I was spending time with Christian friends, involved in "safe" activities, they would assume I was on the right path.

But they had no idea what was really going on.

A study session at a girl friend's house was really a make-out party, where each couple snuck into a different bedroom. A group of friends going to a movie was really an excuse for groping sessions in dark corners of the theater. A get-together at a "Christian" friend's house was really a sex and alcohol fest, with the supervising parents strangely missing. Because of my commitment to purity, I held myself back from certain things, like oral sex or losing my virginity, but I pushed as close to the line as I could.

Sure, I went to youth group and attended plenty of legitimate activities. I studied hard and made good grades. I sang in a girls' choir and joined a drama team. I had girlfriends over to my house for slumber parties, where we did nothing but eat junk food and watch chick flicks. On the outside, I appeared a normal, healthy, well-adjusted teen.

But, like many in the younger generation today, the cost of survival had left me with shameful secrets.

UNDERSTANDING THE BATTLE

Today's young people are in desperate need of parents and leaders who understand the intensity of the battle they are in, and who are equipped to help them discover something better than the cultural norm.

Your child may not be surrounded by the same perversion that I was. He or she may be in a far more sheltered school environment and have friends who are genuinely healthy influences. Your child may even be one of the few in this generation who is living a truly set-apart life.

But even if you are blessed with children who are making godly choices, Eric and I believe that *all* parents need to understand the battle that is raging over the hearts and minds of today's younger generation. We have seen firsthand the vital role that parents and leaders play when it comes to investing in the marriages of tomorrow. But none of us can be equipped to invest in this generation's future until we fully grasp the issues of today.

I recently read a transcript of an *Oprah* show called "The Secret Sex Lives of Teens." Though the content was jarring, it effectively captured the sexual crisis that Eric and I have witnessed among today's young people. Journalist Michelle Buford interviewed over fifty teen girls and their mothers for the show and shared her findings with Oprah.

"It's really shocking, actually," Buford said, reporting that the majority of the girls she talked to—even as young as eleven or twelve years old—confessed to regularly participating in casual sex, orgies, oral sex, and anal sex. Buford reported these activities taking place among teens from seemingly stable family environments. "This is not just a single-parent, inner-city problem," she pointed out.

Buford relayed that the girls she interviewed had no sense of shame in being sexually involved with partners to whom they had no commitment or connection. "[Their attitude is] 'meet me after study hall at four, we'll sleep together,' and then on to the next partner tomorrow. Slam, bam, thank you, ma'am," Buford said.

She admitted that the interview awakened her to a whole new vocabulary. Terms like *salad toss* (oral anal sex), *rainbow party* (where several girls put on lipstick and give oral sex to one or more guys), and *Hoovering* (a girl having an abortion) were commonplace among the teens with whom she spoke. [1]

It is nothing short of heartbreaking when we come face-to-face with how widespread today's sexual crisis really is.

Not long ago someone gave me an article from *Ladies' Home Journal* that said one in twelve children is no longer a virgin by his or her thirteenth birthday and that 21 percent of ninth graders have slept with four or more partners. The author, Lisa Collier Cool, says that even those who remain virgins aren't necessarily innocent, quoting a national survey that found 55 percent of thirteen to nineteen-year-olds admitted to engaging in oral sex.

Even more disturbing are some of the teen sex scandals cropping up around the country. Cool writes about the arrest of a twelve-year-old girl and thirteen-year-old boy for organizing an oral-sex-for-hire ring at a middle school in upper class Reston, Maryland. Another incident took place in suburban Rockland County, Georgia, in which more than two hundred children—some as young as twelve—were exposed to syphilis through group sex. "Local health officials were appalled by reports of fourteen-year-olds with as many as fifty sex partners, and girls who engaged in sexual activities with three boys at once," she writes.[2]

Today's sex-at-thirteen relationships are nothing like the soda-fountain romances of the past; when couples would go to the ice cream shop after school and girls would wear their boyfriends' high school pins. Many in today's younger generation have sworn off boyfriend-girlfriend relationships altogether in exchange for "hooking-up." They prefer sexual encounters with "no-strings-attached." They see emotions and romantic desires as something to be scoffed at.

An article in the *New York Times Magazine*, elaborates on these disturbing trends among modern youth. "[Teens] talk about hookups as matter-of-factly as they might discuss what's on the cafeteria lunch menu—and they look at you in a funny way if you go on for too long about the 'emotional' components of sex," the author says.[3]

As tempting as it might be to deny reality, these horrifying facts demand that we wake up and accept the truth—the soul of today's younger generation is in jeopardy. And it is time that we begin fighting on their behalf.

WHAT ABOUT CHRISTIAN TEENS?

It's easy to assume that such disturbing activities are only taking place among non-Christian teens. But is that a safe assumption? Are things really so different among kids who go to church, hang out with Christian peers, and have a solid support system at home?

Sadly, the answer is often no. Eric and I have spent the past ten years interacting with countless Christian teens around this country. To our dismay, we've observed that many are only one or two steps behind the rest of the world when it comes to sexual compromise, and some have already caught up.

Of course, there are plenty of Christian teens who have *not* succumbed to the sexual pressure of today. There are inestimable benefits that come from a Christian upbringing and a church environment. Eric and I have witnessed some amazing Christian young people who are living set-apart lives amid a perverse generation—not just keeping themselves physically pure, but mentally, emotionally, and spiritually pure as well.

But there are alarmingly few who fall into that category.

Sexual perversion doesn't merely lurk in dark corners as it once did. It isn't prevalent only among drug users and dropouts. It doesn't wait to attack until kids have the maturity to handle it. And it isn't restricted to non-Christian circles.

The longer Eric and I work with the younger generation, the more aware we become of how intense and far-reaching the sexual struggle is for today's Christian young people. We see it in the tormented eyes of teens that ask us for prayer or advice. We hear it in the broken voices of young adults who weep over the trauma and devastation they have experienced from sexual compromise. We read it in the innumerable desperate letters and emails that come to us from kids who have reached their end and don't know where else to turn.

In many cases, the parents of these young people are God-fearing, loving, and supportive, but they are completely in the dark about their child's sexual activities.

Sarah, a fifteen-year-old who is active in her church youth group, shared her story with me in an e-mail last week. "Everyone thinks I am the perfect Christian teen," she writes, "but I feel so far away from God. I lost my virginity when I was thirteen, to a sixteen-year-old guy from my youth group, and I have been sexually active ever since then. My parents have no idea. They still picture me walking down the aisle in a white dress someday. I can't stand my life being such a lie."

Kimber, a fourteen-year-old from California, recently gave me a glimpse of her background through a torrent of tears. "I was raised in a Christian home, but I was sexually molested by my uncle from the age of six," she admitted. "I grew up acting perfect and pious on the outside, but hating myself on the inside, until finally I was so desperate for approval that I let myself be used by one guy after the next. I have been suicidal and anorexic for two years. No one in my life has a clue. I feel like I have already destroyed my life, and I'm not even old enough to drive yet."

Troy, a sixteen-year-old who leads worship at his Christian school, sent Eric a frustrated letter last month. "I have read all the books on purity and even signed an abstinence commitment," he writes, "but I can't live the way God wants me to, no matter how hard I try. I have been involved with three different girls, and it has always ended in sex, oral sex, or both. I am dating someone now, and things have already gone much further than they should. My parents would be devastated if they knew."

Our culture's sexual agenda is aggressive, relentless, and powerful. And today's kids—even many Christian ones—are surrounded by it, engulfed in it, much younger than most of us imagine.

Facing Reality

When I was sixteen, I was asked to speak at a women's tea about the sexual pressure facing modern Christian teens. The ladies were part of a mothers-of-teens prayer group at a local church, and they wanted a young person to tell them what things were really like in high school at that time.

Not wanting to shock anyone, I tried to start with something on the mild side.

"In the halls at school, you hear a lot of perverted jokes and propositions," I told them. "There's also a lot of sexual touching and grabbing—even between guys and girls who barely know each other."

The women looked at me in disbelief. I quickly realized that to them, my words seemed anything but mild.

"You mean, like a boy touching a girl on her knee or something?" ventured one of the moms in an uncertain tone.

I smiled awkwardly. "Uh, no, it's usually a couple feet north of there."

A few of the women exchanged horrified glances.

"Well, why don't the girls say something?" another mom demanded. "I mean, that's sexual harassment! They shouldn't put up with it!"

I hesitated, growing more uncomfortable by the minute. I didn't know how to explain that the girls weren't helpless victims in these situations—most of them actually spurred on or even initiated this kind of sexual attention. And I understood the reason. Even if we were allowing ourselves to become sex objects, at least we could prove that we were attractive and desirable in the eyes of the opposite sex.

Before I had time to formulate a response to the sexual harassment issue, another question was fired my way. "But how many kids are *actually* having sex?" a woman wanted to know. "I mean, don't most of them just act like they are doing it? Isn't it usually just a bunch of talk?"

I looked at the faces of these loving moms. Did they really want the truth?

After a moment's pause, I finally decided to be honest. "Out of my ten closest friends, only four of them are still virgins, even though all of them say they are Christians. And even the ones who are still virgins have done a lot of . . . other stuff." I deftly left out the fact that *I* was among the ones who had done a lot of "other stuff."

A heavy silence filled the room. Most of the women sat shaking their heads in bewilderment.

Finally, one of the women spoke up. "I have a very close relationship with my daughter," she said confidently. "I'm sure she would tell me if she was involved in anything like that."

I looked at the lady who had just spoken. Her daughter was an acquaintance of mine from school, and I knew that she had been physically intimate with at least two guys in the past three months.

As I gazed around the room, I realized that I knew many of the kids these mothers represented. And most of them had made sexual choices that were anything but innocent.

Yet these mothers couldn't bring themselves to believe that their children were capable of deceiving them; that their kids were professing a commitment to purity and then secretly tossing it away. It was so much easier for them to convince each other that *their* children were different, that since they made good grades and attended youth group, they were immune to the sexual crisis of the younger generation.

But sadly, most of them were wrong.

It's easy to assume that when kids are well established in Christianity—attending youth group, going to purity rallies, and dating other Christians—that they are living a set-apart life.

As Eric and I travel the country and interact with parents of teens, we frequently hear statements such as, "My daughter is really active in her youth group, and she only goes out with Christian guys." Or, "My son is dating a girl right now—and they have both signed abstinence commitments."

These parents sincerely believe their children are on the right path, simply because of the Christian influences in their lives. And in some cases, they are right. But it is not uncommon for us to meet the children of these parents later and learn that they are living sexually compromised lifestyles in spite of their Christian surroundings.

Instead of being truly involved and active in their children's spiritual and emotional lives, we've seen many parents choose the easier route: simply making sure their kids go to youth group and hang out with Christian friends and then assuming everything is fine. But in today's world, a Christian label often means little.

When Eric was in high school, he was invited to a youth group party at a friend's house and told to bring money for pizza. His parents gave him the money, happy to see him choose to spend his Friday night with Christian friends. When Eric got to the party, he was surprised to learn that the money was not for pizza; it was for a stripper his friend's dad had hired for their evening entertainment. This was a group of so-called Christian guys, the party being hosted by so-called Christian parents. But their true colors became shockingly clear that night.

A seventeen-year-old girl recently wrote me an e-mail, confessing to having a secret sexual relationship with her youth pastor. A young man from a Christian school told us that he knew of only two virgins in his graduating class of more than one hundred.

Parents who assume that "Christian" equates to purity are in for a rude awakening.

MODERN YOUTH GROUP CULTURE

I attended youth group for the first time when I was thirteen.

It was during the same period of my life when I was struggling to deal with the perversion and pressure I faced at school each day. I didn't think my parents could ever understand the reality of my world, and I had begun to shut them out. I was desperate for someone who would empathize with what I was going through. And that night, sitting in the youth room listening to Kevin, our attractive twenty-three-year-old youth pastor, I thought I might have found what I was looking for.

"I know what you guys are going through," Kevin said sincerely, looking at us with his intense blue eyes. "I'm young, and I can relate to your world." He flashed us a smile with his perfect teeth. "Hey, your mom and dad mean well, but they are kind of out-of-touch with reality, am I right?"

A murmur of agreement rumbled among the kids as one of the guys yelled out, "Right on, man!"

Then Kevin's face grew serious. "I know that not a single one of you in this room actually has a good relationship with your parents," he said. "I mean, lots of you hate your parents' guts." Kevin's mouth curved sarcastically. "If anyone in here can honestly say that they actually *like* spending time with their parents," he looked each of us in the eye, "then I want you to raise your hand right now."

Silence filled the youth room. I shifted nervously in my seat. To me, Kevin's words seemed harsh. Sure, I'd had trouble communicating with my parents lately, but I certainly wouldn't go as far as saying I couldn't stand being around them. Up until recently, they had been my closest friends. Suddenly, I found myself wanting to challenge Kevin's bold statement, to raise my hand and tell him that I loved and respected my parents, that I wasn't just another typical rebellious teenager.

But one glance around me at the haughty faces of the guys and the arrogant smirks of the girls, and I knew I should keep my mouth shut. This was not a safe environment. Even Kevin, our ever-sensitive youth pastor, seemed to be waiting to pounce mercilessly on any of us who tried to argue with him.

When no one responded to Kevin's question, he sat back in his chair with a satisfied look on his face. "Just as I thought," he said triumphantly. "You guys go through hell every day, and your parents are clueless. But don't worry about it. Even though you can't talk to Mom and Dad anymore, that's what your youth leaders are here for."

At thirteen, I lived in a world where survival was all that mattered. My chief concern was making it through the next five years without being targeted for rejection. And to do that, I needed to fit in. I desperately wanted to be normal. According to Kevin, and seemingly everyone else, being normal meant having a terrible relationship with my parents. So that's what I strove to become—a "normal" Christian teen who was constantly at war with the two people who had once been my best friends.

Before I started attending youth group, my relationship with my parents had been strained, though still caring and loving. But after a few weeks of Kevin's pep talks, I began to push them away with every ounce of my being. My relationship with them went from tense to completely nonexistent in a matter of a few months. And soon I felt just like one of the other teens that couldn't stand being in the same room with their parents.

But a tumultuous home life was not the only thing that was expected in my youth group environment. The longer I spent in Christian youth culture, the more I learned that to be normal was to be a young person who was constantly teetering on the edge of the moral fence.

During a youth group series on "Love, Sex, and Dating," a burly sophomore named Jason voiced the question that was secretly burning on all of our hearts. "Uh . . . yeah, man," he muttered awkwardly, staring at the floor with a red face, "I was just wondering . . . like, how far is too far? I mean, what kind of physical stuff is, like, okay with God?"

Unconsciously, we all leaned forward, eager to hear Kevin's response. Most of us in the room, myself included, had done things with the opposite sex that we felt guilty about. Because of the endless lectures on abstinence we received, the importance of saving sex until marriage to avoid pregnancy and STDs was drilled into our minds. And as a result, many of us had retained our technical virginity. But for the majority of us, that's all it was—*technical* virginity. What Jason was really asking that day was, "Is it a sin to become physical with someone, as long as you are still a virgin when you get married?"

I never forgot Kevin's answer. He leaned back in his chair with a smile and paused thoughtfully.

"There's really no right answer to that question," he finally said. "I mean, everyone has different boundaries. When you are with your boyfriend or girlfriend, and things start to heat up between you, it's just important that you stop whenever you start to feel uncomfortable." He winked at us knowingly. "Hey, God knows we're only human. It's normal to have physical contact with the opposite sex. Just make sure that you don't let it get out of control."

According to Kevin, everything I had done with guys in dark corners of parties or movie theaters was okay in God's eyes, because I hadn't let things get out of control or given up my virginity. But somehow, his words didn't make me feel any less guilty about the way I was living.

I went to several different youth groups throughout my teen years. And when it came to purity, each of them seemed to convey the same subtle message: "You can be 'normal' and be a Christian at the same time. You can approach dating and relationships the same way everyone else does, just try to hang on to those last shreds of your purity as best you can."

There were Sunday school lessons entitled, "How to Avoid Ending up in the Back Seat of the Car on Friday Night's Hot Date." Unfortunately, the answer presented did *not* involve simply avoiding that situation in the first place. There were small group discussions on break-up recovery. The few who had not yet experienced a serious relationship and break-up were made to feel like oddities, despite the fact that everyone there was under the age of sixteen. And then there was the constant question from my youth pastors and small group leaders: "So, Leslie, do you have a boyfriend?" I dreaded having to answer that question if they happened to catch me in between boyfriends. Being unattached quickly put me in the "abnormal teen" category. Even in Christian circles, I felt intense pressure to be accepted and approved.

Though my parents had sent me to youth group in hopes that it would be a positive influence on me, in truth it accomplished little, if anything, of spiritual substance in my life. In fact, looking back, it is easy to see that the influence was far more negative than positive. The more embroiled I became in Christian youth culture, the more I allowed the voices of shallow youth leaders like Kevin to become my excuses for living a deluded and compromised existence.

Too many Christian young people today are finding themselves in that same boat.

"CHRISTIAN" VS. SET APART

Does this mean that all youth group environments are dangerous? Not at all. There are many exceptions to what I experienced growing up. Eric and I have met many spiritually vibrant youth leaders who are pouring out their lives to help young people discover the reality of Christ.

To fight for the younger generation, we need more leaders like these. We need to team up with leaders who are willing to challenge our young people to a higher standard—the standard of Jesus Christ.

There is a common assumption among many Christian youth leaders that modern-day teens are not truly capable of discovering a cutting-edge relationship with Christ. They often water down truth in order to appeal to the "largest common denominator": the kids who profess to be Christians, but are constantly struggling with the most basic moral issues. There is rarely an allowance made for the possibility that Christian teens are capable of more.

Cassie is a young woman who has chosen to stay out of the dating scene, ignore the popularity ladder, and instead use her teen years to serve Christ in practical ways. She is a beautiful, confident, and spiritually solid girl. But at her church, she is often ignored and isolated by the youth leaders. The lessons and messages never seem to apply to her; they seem to merely cater to those struggling with morality. When her parents mentioned this to her youth pastor, he replied, "Well, I'm sorry she feels that way, but you can't expect us to customize things for your daughter. If she isn't struggling with the same things everyone else is, then she is totally abnormal."

But the reality is that there are thousands of teens like Cassie around this country, just waiting for someone to present them with the true standard of Christ. Eric and I encounter them continually. They are longing to live on the cutting edge; to radically give themselves to the King of kings, to live lives that are anything but "normal."

Yet many are never offered that chance.

The solution to our culture's sex-at-thirteen crisis is not to simply spit out more "Christian" young people, teens who know all the Bible stories but live deluded and compromised lives. We don't need a generation of typical Christian young people. We need a generation of *set-apart* young people, those who allow every aspect of their existence to be radically transformed by the grace and power of Jesus Christ.

HOPE ON THE HORIZON

The concept of a set-apart generation may seem like an impossible dream in light of today's sex-at-thirteen culture. But as important as it is to realize the intensity of the battle, it is also vital to realize that hope is far from lost.

I know from firsthand experience.

Throughout those rocky teen years, when my life was racked with compromise, my parents prayed diligently that God would show me a better way—a higher way. And God answered their request, far beyond what they would have ever dreamed.

When I was sixteen, a radical change took place in my heart and life. I began to hear God's soft, beckoning voice, calling me away from the diluted Christian existence I had settled for. He began to draw me back to Himself, to convict me of my sin, and to give me strength to turn and walk a different way.

One spring day, in the middle of my sophomore year of high school, I surrendered my entire life to Him. I had acknowledged Christ as my Savior from an early age. But now, I gave Him my entire existence. I gave Him the pen of my life and asked Him to script my story in any way He desired. No longer was purity just an abstinence commitment or "Christian rule" I forced myself to obey. Purity was the outflow of a fully set-apart life—a life totally yielded to the God of the universe.

Every area of my life began to radically change. Instead of pursuing shallow popularity, I began to pursue Jesus Christ with all my heart. Instead of building my life around the pursuit of the opposite sex, I began to build my life around the King of kings. And instead of keeping my parents at arm's length, I invited them to be my teammates. They became my faithful prayer and accountability partners, two of my closest friends. And they played an instrumental role in my love story with Eric.

I have never regretted my decision to allow the God of the universe to overtake my existence. When I gave Him the pen of my life, He was more faithful than I ever could have dreamed or imagined. He wrote for me a story far more amazing and fulfilling than any Hollywood drama ever made.

My story of hope isn't the only one out there. As Eric and I have traveled this country during the past decade, we've seen more and more young people who are choosing to give God the pen of their lives. And just like us, they are experiencing the wonder of a God-scripted *life* story and the beauty of a God-written *love* story.

Set-apart young people aren't as rare as they used to be. A few years ago, Eric and I received a call from a reporter for NBC's *Dateline*. "There seems to be a 'purity revival' that is taking place among young people around this country," the reporter said. "We were wondering if you could tell us more about it."

In the midst of a generation enslaved to sexual perversion and compromise, something incredible is taking place— something so baffling that even the secular media is taking notice. Out of the ashes of our culture's sexual holocaust, a different breed of young people is emerging. They are those who make completely different choices than their young counterparts, those who choose to live a set-apart life in a generation that holds nothing sacred.

These few are not the ones who merely make abstinence commitments or wear promise rings. Rather, they are those who obey their King with radical abandon, those who live faithfully for Him and for their future spouse with every ounce of their heart, soul, mind, and body.

Every Christian young person is meant to be among these few. Whether your child is already on this path or as far from it as possible, you play a vital role in transforming our sex-at-thirteen generation into a *set-apart* generation. Hope is on the horizon. Together, let's explore the incredible opportunity that each of us has to begin investing today in the marriages of tomorrow.

In a Nutshell

Our culture's sexual agenda is aggressive, relentless, and powerful. And today's kids—even many Christian ones—are surrounded by it and engulfed in it, much younger than most of us imagine.

Sexual perversion doesn't merely lurk in dark corners as it once did. It isn't prevalent only among drug users and dropouts. It doesn't wait to attack until kids have the maturity to handle it. And it isn't restricted to non-Christian circles.

The soul of today's younger generation is in serious jeopardy. And it is time that we begin fighting on their behalf.

Today's young people are in desperate need of parents and leaders who understand the intensity of the battle they are in, and who are equipped to help them discover something better than the cultural norm.

It is nothing short of heartbreaking when we come face-to-face with how widespread today's sexual crisis really is. However, *to see it* and *to accept it* are two very different things. As dark as the problem facing our children today is, the light of God's amazing solution is far more intense.

Satan may have an agenda to destroy your child, but God has an agenda to see your child discover His highest and best. As a parent, you play the defining role that determines the final outcome of this great drama. You are the wild card! The question this book poses isn't "What will your child choose?" but rather, "What will you choose for your child?"

Part One

A Vision for Something Better

As for God, his way is perfect.
—Psalm 18:30 (NKJV)

❖

*For as the heavens are higher than
the earth, so are my ways higher
than your ways.*
—Isaiah 55:9

❖

*Thy way, O God, is holy.
What god is great like our God?*
—Psalm 77:13 (NASB)

❖

1

Beyond Broken Promise Rings

*Giving the sex-at-thirteen generation
a vision for something better*

Eric

AS PARENTS AND LEADERS, how should we respond to the crisis of today's sex-at-thirteen generation? How can we protect our children from being scathed by the unrelenting perversion that swirls around them? How can we motivate them to pursue something better?

Is now the time to panic, to take our kids out of modern society and frantically shelter them every form of sexual pollution in our culture?

Should we scare them into making the right choices, bombarding them with frightening statistics about pregnancy and STDs? Should we load them down with rules and regulations to follow? Should we hover over them protectively and keep them on a super-tight leash?

Or is there a better way?

THE SIREN ALLUREMENT

Greek mythology tells of a certain group of evil, conniving mermaids—the Sirens. These mermaids, though spectacular in beauty, were devilish and diabolical. Their weapon was the intoxicating song that they sang. Sitting atop their rocks, the Sirens would sing their tempting tune as ships passed. It was a powerful enticement that no hot-blooded man could resist. With their lustful melody, the Sirens could control the wills of men. Their song could woo even the most steely hearted ship captains to turn their vessels toward the Siren's rocky coastline. Their music lured ship after ship into a watery grave.

Enter Ulysses—a ship captain of great renown whose noble mission forces him to pass those terrible Siren shores. But Ulysses is determined that he will not fall victim to their allurement as so many others have done. So as he approaches the deadly Siren coastline, he commands his crew to stuff beeswax in their ears so they won't be overcome by the haunting songs.

Ulysses himself is intrigued to hear the music that has sent so many mighty sailors to their death. But he knows he cannot withstand the temptation. So he commands his crew to tie him to the mast of the ship, and tie him tight. He reasons that he can safely listen to the Sirens' song while bound to the mast since the ropes will render him unable to steer his ship in the wrong direction.

As the intoxicating Siren melody fills the air, Ulysses is overcome with uncontrollable longing to steer his ship toward their dangerous shore. His knees buckle and his mind swoons under the sway of the Siren sounds. He screams for his crew to turn the boat toward the singing, but his crew is already under orders not to heed his voice while he is under the mermaids' spell.

Ulysses curses, writhing in agony, consumed with only one thought—*"I must get closer to the music! I must quench this insatiable thirst for more of the Sirens' song!"* He furiously seeks to untie the ropes that bind him. But his efforts are useless, and he shakes in misery until finally the mermaid music fades to nothingness and his ship sails beyond its terrifying reach.

When the danger is past, Ulysses is untied. He falls to the deck of the ship, exhausted and humiliated by the entire episode.

And yet, Ulysses is a hero. He did what few had ever done before him—he made it past the temptation. He escaped death upon the rocks.

His crew applauds their strong and noble captain for his amazing feat. He succeeded in escaping danger in spite of the fact that *he was miserable the entire time.*[1]

TIED TO THE MAST

Ulysses' story captures my growing-up years in a nutshell. Like an entire generation of young Christians today, I kept sailing past the Siren coastline while tied to the mast.

I was a virgin when I graduated from high school. While that wasn't something to brag about in my circle of guy friends, my abstinence educators were beside themselves with joy—pronouncing me a grand success. I was certainly a rarity in my generation. I hadn't caved to the pressure and given away my physical purity. I hadn't put myself at risk for getting a girl pregnant or for contracting an STD. I made it past the danger.

But I was miserable the entire time.

Inwardly, I hated that stupid mast, and I despised the ropes that held me there. I even resented the fact that it was the God-prescribed "good thing" for me to avoid crashing into those crazy rocks. I actually *wanted* to crash—to experience what everyone else was experiencing. I wanted to get closer to the music.

> Time and time again, I wished I hadn't been brought up in a Christian home with Christian morals. Everyone else had the freedom to give in to temptation.

Time and time again, I wished I hadn't been brought up in a Christian home with Christian morals. Everyone else had the freedom to give in to temptation. They recklessly steered toward the Siren coastline and satisfied their cravings, while I was forced to listen to the intoxicating melody from a distance, bound by rules and restrictions.

Like Ulysses, I made it, but I was miserable.

In youth group I received pep talks on "Enduring Rope Burn," and "Trying to Find Joy in the Mast." I heard messages on "The Dangers of the Sirens' Shoreline" and on "Choosing Not to Let the Music Get to You."

But in clandestine meetings, when parents and leaders weren't around, we Christians teens would examine loopholes in the rope system and chart ways to bring our love boats as close to the rocks as possible without puncturing the sides.

The Ulysses model only bred an attitude of "How close is too close?" I was constantly trying to inch my ship closer and closer to the Sirens' song. I was always trying to experience as much of the Sirens' melody as possible without actually going "all the way" into the danger zone.

PURE MISERY

The typical Christian model for true love training today is pure misery. It offers nothing but beeswax and ropes to help us make it past the enticing Siren shores. It doesn't give us a vision for anything more than a miserable ride through tempting waters.

Christian young people are exposed to plenty of books, lectures, pep talks, and paraphernalia about the importance of saving sex until marriage. But while the abstinence message might help prevent teen pregnancy and STDs, it falls short of offering the sex-at-thirteen generation the hope and vision they are desperately seeking.

Though I managed to navigate my way through my young adult years with my "technical" virginity intact, in reality my life was far from pure. The culture's sexual agenda attacked me at a young age, awakening me to my sexuality long before I should have ever been alert to such things. Sex education classes, the media, and my buddies' twisted insights helped me understand what normal male behavior looked like—fascination with the female body and only "one thing" on the mind. And what young man doesn't want to be normal, especially when *that* is the definition of normal?

I knew what God said about such a distorted mentality, but the attraction to sex was too much for me to resist. I justified my behavior by telling myself, "Well, at least I'm not having sex. So what if I am addicted to pornography? I'm doing my good deed by not getting girls pregnant and cheating on my future wife."

The Christian message drew a line in the sand—*don't have sex*. Don't crash your ship on the rocky Siren coastline. I felt that as long as I didn't technically give away my virginity, then God would be proud of me, or at least content with my behavior. So everything *up* to the Siren coastline became my water to explore. I could listen to the Sirens' music and get as close to their song as possible, just as long as I didn't actually crash upon the rocks.

And when I graduated, I was a hero in the abstinence movement—a trophy. I proved that a young man could make it through high school with his purity intact.

But strangely, by the end of it all, I didn't feel pure. I felt dirty. I felt as if I had lost something precious, though I didn't know what it was. Like Ulysses, I was exhausted, humiliated, and miserable from the whole experience.

Not long ago, Leslie and I attended a Christian event where some young people were being honored for an "outstanding achievement." Their accomplishment? They had made it through high school without having sex. They had maintained an abstinence commitment in the midst of sexual pressure.

These young people received a standing ovation and roaring applause. As far as the parents and leaders were concerned, these teens were the epitome of Christian purity. But it was merely their commitment to physical abstinence that set these teens apart. As Leslie and I had the opportunity to look closer at their lives, it was obvious that they weren't living much differently than their secular teen counterparts.

Is this what we want for the up-and-coming generation?

Should we cheer on young men, though they are addicted to pornography and treat girls as sex objects, just as long as they remain technical virgins? Should we cheer on young women, who, though they maintain the shell of physical purity, have given their heart away to twenty young men by the age of eighteen?

Do we desire for our children only the shell of purity while all the beautiful substance within drains into nothingness? Is God's desire for His children only that we don't have sex before we marry? Is that really the secret to a lasting love?

Not even close! There is so much more to it!

Unless the abstinence message is part of a bigger vision—a vision of an amazing marriage, a glorious picture of happily-ever-after romance that stands the tests of time—then it is nothing but a Band-Aid covering up a deadly cancerous growth. Rules and moral boundaries are nothing more than ropes, tying kids to the mast so they don't crash their ship, making them miserable the entire time.

The sex-at-thirteen generation needs more.

Singing a Sweeter Song

Greek legend has it that there was another noble captain who braved the lurid waters of the Sirens. In fact, he wasn't far behind Ulysses. His name was Orpheus. And his approach to the Siren threat was very different than that of Ulysses. He didn't use beeswax, and he didn't use rope. He wasn't afraid of the Sirens. He looked upon the dangerous coastline as an opportunity.

As his ship approached the Siren enticement, his crew let out a shout of joy.

"The Sirens! The Sirens! Captain Orpheus, it is time!"

While Ulysses' crew had been filled with dread as they approached this legendary danger, Orpheus's crew was buoyant with excitement. Some, in fact, had joined Orpheus's crew just for this very occasion.

"Bring me the case!" boomed Orpheus, as the sailors cheered.

A beautifully adorned case was brought to Orpheus. He smiled as he opened it. The crew surrounded him, their eyes filled with eager anticipation. Orpheus slowly removed from the case a lovely musical instrument, studded with jewels and plated with precious metals.

"Play it, Captain!" roared the crew, as their eyes transfixed upon their hero. "Play us your song!"

As the Sirens' sweet melody began to fill the air, Orpheus began to play his own instrument. It was the most perfect music human ears had ever heard. Each crewman became lost in the grandeur and majesty of the song.

All too soon the Siren coastline was out of sight and the master musician concluded the song that he himself had composed. Not a single man aboard ship had been tempted by the Sirens' melody. In fact, no one even noticed it. Though the mermaids' music was alluring and sweet, Orpheus played for his crew . . . *a sweeter song.*[2]

Today's young people don't need more lectures on how to tie themselves to the mast. They don't need more lessons on the dangers of the Siren coastline. Our kids don't need more pep talks on how to make it through high school with their virginity intact.

The younger generation needs *a sweeter song.*

A God-built romance isn't merely a "moral version" of the

culture's mediocre love stories. God doesn't need to imitate the world's way of building a relationship; *He has His own way.* Like Captain Orpheus, God sings a sweeter song. It's a song so breathtaking and satisfying that it makes the alluring melody of the Sirens no more appealing than an obnoxious foghorn.

And when young people hear even a strain of God's glorious melody, when they catch a glimpse of the spectacular beauty of a God-scripted love story, they are willing to do whatever it takes in order to experience it for themselves. No longer will they need constant pep-talks and scare tactics to avoid the sexual temptation of the culture. When they truly understand the fulfillment and wonder of God's ways, they are no longer overcome by the Sirens' alluring music. They have heard a sweeter song.

Ten years ago, Leslie and I were asked to share our love story with several hundred teens. It was the first time we had presented a message on guy/girl relationships to young people, and we had no idea what to expect. As we entered the stage and surveyed the crowd, knots began to form in our stomachs. The young people seemed anything but eager to be there. They stared at us defiantly, many of them draped around a member of the opposite sex, some of them passionately kissing their boyfriends or girlfriends. It seemed that a message on "seeking God's best" in relationships was the last thing this group wanted to hear.

But a change came over the teens as we began to talk. We shared with them the amazing beauty of what we had discovered: a love story scripted by the Author of romance Himself. We gave them a glimpse into the wonder and fulfillment of God's ways. And instead of telling them all the things they couldn't do—all the rules and boundaries and restrictions they were used

> The primary reason that young people give in to the sexual temptation of the culture is that they don't believe there is anything better to wait for.

to hearing—we shared with them what they *could* do. We passed on a vision of something so much more incredible than anything they had ever seen or heard. And by the end of the evening, nearly the entire crowd was on their faces, weeping, repenting of their compromised lives, and making heartfelt commitments to choose a different path.

Nearly every group of young people that Leslie and I have spoken to over the past decade has responded as that first group did. The younger generation is urgently seeking hope. When we offer them a vision for something better, when we point them to God's sweeter song, they are willing to do whatever it takes in order to experience it for themselves.

SHIFTING THE FOCUS

As Christian parents and leaders, it is tempting to become overwhelmed by the danger of the Sirens. We frantically devise new ways to tie our kids to the mast, frantic to keep them from crashing on the rocky shores of sexual compromise. But when this becomes our focus, we fail to offer the younger generation what they *really* need . . . a vision for something better.

The primary reason that young people give in to the sexual temptation of the culture is that they don't believe there is anything better to wait for. They don't know there is a sweeter song.

The Christian community frequently reminds the younger generation that "true love waits." But most of today's young people don't believe that true love can ever be found. Why wait for something that doesn't exist?

Kyle, a disillusioned high school sophomore, shared his perspective on relationships with me not long ago. "I think that true love is a joke," he said. "My parents hate each others' guts. I don't know one married couple that's happy. I'm not going to waste my life waiting around for something that's not even real."

Madison, an insecure nineteen-year-old, sent us a desperate e-mail asking, "Can true love really exist anymore? I keep settling for jerks who are only interested in one thing, because I can't imagine someone ever really loving me for a lifetime."

Where is this hopelessness coming from?

Sadly, it often comes from the very sources that should be imparting vision to a generation in crisis. It often comes from the older generation.

Just before Leslie and I got married, we were attacked by several gigantic "wet blankets," doing their best to snuff out any vision we might have for a happily-ever-after love story.

"So, you're getting married, huh?" they would smirk when they saw the engagement ring. "Are you really ready for the old ball-and-chain?"

"Let me give you some advice," they would say when they saw our excitement. "Soak up the romance while you can—it won't be around for long!"

When these wet blankets fall on a young life, it is difficult to aim toward something better. And too often the wet blankets are thrown by well-meaning Christians.

It's difficult to expect more out of love and marriage when everyone around you tells you there's nothing more to find. It's difficult to expend the energy training to be great in a future marriage when you are told that marriages all turn out the same. And it's especially difficult, when you are young and virile, to sacrifice the sensual pleasures of the here-and-now for a romantically challenged version of marriage somewhere in the unforeseeable future.

Leslie and I represent a generation in dire need of vision—a generation that does not understand what true love is even supposed to look like.

> Today's sex-at-thirteen generation typically feels that it's a waste of time to invest in their future love story, because the idea of lasting love seems distant and far-fetched.

The younger generation isn't blind. They notice the lack of sparkle in married couples' eyes. They observe the fighting. They hear the harsh, demeaning words. They take note of the lack of beauty, tenderness, and romance. They see the divorce papers.

Very few have ever seen even one marriage that would cause them to say, "When I get married, I want my marriage to be exactly like *that!*"

Today's sex-at-thirteen generation typically feels that it's a waste of time to invest in their future love story, because the idea of lasting love seems distant and far-fetched. All that matters is making it through today. They don't wait around for long-term relationships; they live in a world of temporary flings and one-night stands.

And even those who have been brought up with Christian values are often tempted to settle for short-term gratification, because they believe it is a waste of time to wait for more.

Leslie and I were told about a poll that was taken among the younger generation, asking what their greatest desire in life was. At the top of the li   r most was the desire to be married to one person for a lif ne. But when asked if they really believed that kind of lasting love was possible, a huge majority of the young people said no.

It is no longer enough to tell young people they should wait for something better. They first need to believe that something better really exists. And we, as parents and leaders, must be the ones to pass on that vision.

Raising the Bar

I've always been a singer. I'm not always a very good one, but I've always loved to howl out my favorite tunes. When I was nineteen, I wanted to be a *great* singer. But one thing stood in my way—I didn't know how to sing. I tried to teach myself to sing, but as my mother would readily tell you, it wasn't a very pleasant experience for everyone else at the Ludy home. I tried to mimic the raspy voice of Joe Cocker or the high squeal of Steve Perry. But no matter how hard I tried, I still sounded like a Muppet with laryngitis.

The reason for my vocal mishaps? I was never *trained* in the art of singing. I'd never had a master of vocal technique take me under his wing and help me understand *practically* how to develop my voice. I needed someone with a vision bigger than my own. I needed someone who could show me how to get from miserable to marvelous.

I'll never forget my first month studying under my vocal coach, Scott.

I couldn't believe how much more there was to vocal training than my pitiful little understanding of singing. In fact, nearly everything I thought about singing was completely wrong. When I would demonstrate my technique, Scott would roll his eyes and moan, "We have to rebuild you from scratch!" I was shocked at how much was required of me, how much time and energy I would need to invest in order to become a great singer. I could hardly fathom how many little things in my body I needed to train just to build a foundation for success.

Since that first day with Scott, I have spent fourteen years training in the art of singing. I will quickly admit that I haven't reached the status of "great singer." I have not yet mastered Captain Orpheus's amazing musical abilities. However, I know what it takes. I have a clear understanding now of how much work is involved in becoming a vocal master.

How many young people find themselves in the same predicament I was in at the age of nineteen? But instead of desiring to be great singers, they want to be great lovers. They want to have a beautiful, fulfilling love story. *They want to sing the sweeter song.*

But like me, they attempt to figure it out on their own. They assume they know the basics of love, through their observation, and they give their best shot at imitating Hollywood's love dramas. They try to kiss like Brad Pitt and flirt like Jennifer Aniston.

But they'll never become great attempting something they don't understand. Nearly everything they think they know about love is wrong.

Just as I had to be completely rebuilt in the art of singing, today's younger generation needs to be *completely rebuilt* in the art of true love. We can't just give them a few rules to follow and expect them to emerge into godly spouses. Just as I had to devote myself to hard work and training in order to excel in singing, we must show the younger generation what it means to *train and prepare for heaven-scripted love.*

The younger generation will never reach the echelons of great love through abstinence commitments alone, any more than I could reach the echelons of great singing through squawking out love songs in the shower.

Today's young people need to understand how grand and beautiful married love can be. They need to realize how much is required of them and how much of themselves they will need to invest if they are to make it to such heights. *They need someone to train them for greatness.* They need someone with a vision bigger than their own.

They need you.

You might be feeling like you yourself need to be trained in the art of godly love before you can possibly pass on a vision to someone else. That's one reason we have written this book. We want to pass on practical tools that will help you impart a vision of lasting love to the younger generation, even if you haven't experienced it in your own life.

A middle-aged married couple recently attended a beautiful wedding. The bride and groom had kept themselves truly pure—heart, mind, and body—for each other. The newlyweds were entering marriage with a solid foundation for love to last a lifetime. As the couple watched the purity and freshness of this new union, they were filled with regret over their own past mistakes.

But instead of focusing on what they had lost, they realized that they had a golden opportunity. "We realized that we can help our son and daughter discover something so much better than the path we chose in our younger years," they told us. They realized that they could become a "steppingstone" to help the next generation reach the heights of God's very best.

As Christian parents and leaders, we have the opportunity to become steppingstones for the next generation—to help them discover something far better than most of us have experienced.

Let's stop tying kids to the mast. Let's give them more than rope and earplugs to fight against the deadly Siren coastline. Let's introduce them to the sweeter song.

In a Nutshell

Abstinence messages just don't cut it! It is no longer enough to tell young people they should wait for something better in their romantic relationships. They first need to believe that something better really exists. They need to understand how grand and beautiful married love can be. They must be given a picture of how perfect a love story can be when God is the one writing it. And, as parents and leaders, you must be the ones to pass on that vision—*the vision of a sweeter song.*

A God-built romance isn't merely a "moral version" of the culture's mediocre love stories. God doesn't need to imitate the world's way of building a relationship; *He has His own way.* Like Captain Orpheus, God sings a sweeter song. It's a song so breathtaking and satisfying that it makes the alluring melody of the Sirens no more appealing than an obnoxious foghorn.

And when young people hear even a strain of God's glorious melody, when they catch a glimpse of the spectacular beauty of a God-scripted love story, they are willing to do whatever it takes in order to experience it for themselves. No longer will they need constant pep talks and scare tactics to avoid the sexual temptation of the culture. When they truly understand the fulfillment and wonder of God's ways, they are no longer overcome by the Sirens' alluring music . . . they have heard a sweeter song.

2

BECOMING A TRUE-LOVE TEAMMATE

The crucial role parents play in their child's future love story.

Eric

STRANGE DECISIONS

MY LOVE STORY WITH LESLIE was odd from the beginning. We made many strange decisions along the way, decisions that no one else around us made. And yet, it was those strange decisions that led us to the sweeter song.

Long before we met, God began laying the foundation for our unusual romance.

I was eighteen when God began to set my life apart. Back then I was your every-day, run-of-the-mill Christian young person; basically moral on the outside and polluted with sexual preoccupation and addiction on the inside. And then I encountered the God of the universe. My life has never been the same.

Up until that point, I had always known *about* God, but I had never allowed God to access my life. I had never relinquished the pen of my life, so that He could begin writing my story. I had always been the one in control. I preferred it that way.

I considered myself a solid Christian. But in reality, I had never given myself to the God of the Bible. I had always served a god of my own making—one that did what I wanted, one that served my personal agenda; one that would give me heaven when I died and one that asked for, well, nothing much in return.

> I considered myself a solid Christian. But in reality, I had never given myself to the God of the Bible. I had always served a god of my own making.

The God of the Bible was a whole new discovery for me. He asked for my *entire life*. He requested everything. And in return He promised that He would fill me with His very life in exchange for my own. He promised that He would take control and do things with my life that were impossible otherwise—beautiful things, powerful things, amazing things. I gave my life to this God. I offered Him the pen of my existence and allowed Him to script my life story from that day on. He began to take over every aspect of my life—even my love life.

He began to change me. He began to train me how to look at women differently, to see them as He sees them. He began to alter my behavior patterns, my thinking patterns, and even my dreams and desires. He was rebuilding me.

And that's when I began to make strange decisions.

For instance, I decided that I wouldn't date another girl until I knew she was to be my wife. At the age of nineteen, that was a scary proposition. But God was giving me a desire to give myself wholly to one woman, to wait for her, and to cherish her even before I ever met her.

God began to teach me not to flirt and draw attention to myself, but to use my life to draw attention to Him. I still was very much attracted to girls, but I was learning how to discipline my mind against harmful thoughts and self-indulgent fantasies. I was learning to honor girls and think of them as my sisters.

Time passed. I was becoming a new man through and through.

I prayed for my future wife every night. I wrote her love letters, telling her that I was faithfully setting my life aside for her alone. I wrote her love songs, expressing my excitement for the time God would bring our lives together. I endeavored to be fully set apart for Christ and fully set apart for my future spouse. It was a lonely time, a challenging time—but the most fulfilling time of my life. I was learning what it truly meant to build my existence around the God of the universe.

A couple of years later, Leslie came into my life. She was beautiful, radiant for Christ, a true princess. She had given God the pen of her life, just as I had done. Over time we became dear friends. We shared a common passion for Christ, a common love for music, and a common desire to pour our lives out in service to our King. We could talk for hours about Scripture and about God's kingdom. There was an incredible spiritual like-mindedness between us that I hadn't found in many other friendships.

Leslie was five years younger than me. Because of that glaring age difference, I didn't entertain the thought of a future with Leslie. I simply enjoyed being around her and thought of her as a younger sister.

As time passed, I grew more and more concerned about my friendship with Leslie. I deeply respected this girl. I thought she was gorgeous both inside and out, but I kept reminding myself that she was five years younger than me.

Eric, I thought to myself, *What if your future wife comes into your life right now? Would she feel comfortable if she saw how much time you are spending with this young girl named Leslie?*

And Eric? the thought continued, *What if Leslie's future husband came into her life right now? How would he be feeling about his girl hanging out with the likes of you?*

I didn't know the answers to these perplexing questions. All I knew is that I wanted to honor my future wife, and I wanted to honor Leslie's future husband.

That's when I made another strange decision. *I decided to meet with Leslie's dad.* I figured if anyone would speak straight with me on this point, it would be him. I wanted answers, even if they were blunt and hard to hear.

THE SACRED TRUST

Rich and I got together at Perkins' Restaurant for lunch one Sunday afternoon. I'll never forget that meeting. Awkwardness swirled in my gut like a rabid butterfly.

"Uh, Rich," I said, to kick off the odd conversation. "I'm concerned about my relationship with Leslie."

I didn't want Rich to think that I was about to ask for his daughter's hand in marriage. The "I'm concerned" line was very strategic in my attempts to pop that elephant-sized balloon hovering over our booth.

I talked for what must have been ten minutes, babbling

uncomfortably about my concerns regarding my future wife and my concerns regarding Leslie's future husband. I'm not sure if I even made any sense.

Finally I was forced to take a breath. In that brief moment, in which I inhaled, Rich slipped into the conversation.

"Eric," he said quietly, "do you know the reason that I know your relationship with my daughter is from God?"

I stared back at him with a quizzical gaze and shook my head.

"Because," he continued, "ever since you have been in Leslie's life, she has grown closer and closer to Jesus Christ."

This was definitely not the kind of correction I had been expecting. And Rich didn't stop there.

"And do you know the reason," he continued, "that I'm confident your relationship with my daughter is pure?"

I swallowed hard, and squeaked out the words, "Uh, how?"

"Because," he said with a mischievous twinkle in his eyes, "if it wasn't pure . . . God would tell me."

God would tell him? My mind was struck dumb with a holy fear.

It was the first time in my life that I recognized the power and reach of parenting. Growing up in the public schools and being separated into peer clusters, I had begun to interpret life outside the grid of family. My friends and I had always acted as if we didn't even have families whenever we were at school. I had always seen young people as Lone Rangers, rather than lives that belonged to family spheres—children under their parents' authority structure.

But through Rich's statement, a whole new world opened up to me. I suddenly recognized that Leslie wasn't just a lone and independent individual. She was a life under authority. She was her dad's princess. God had anointed, appointed, and commissioned Rich to protect his daughter, to provide for her physically, emotionally, and spiritually. Leslie was his treasure—his sacred trust.

Rich was, in essence, saying, "Eric, if you ever tried to go around me, if you tried to access Leslie's heart without honoring my position in her life . . . I would know."

I realized with startling clarity that it was my responsibility to honor that sacred trust over Leslie's life—to respect Rich's God-given position in every way.

As I was pondering this revelation, Rich said something else that caught me completely off guard.

"Eric," he said solemnly, "I give you my blessing to pursue a relationship with my daughter in any way that God leads you."

I started to argue, to clarify to Rich that I wasn't after a romantic relationship with his daughter. But Rich simply held up his hand to curb my explanation.

"I know that's not what you were looking for in this conversation," he said, "but I feel that God wants me to give you that blessing."

God used the words of this man named Rich Runkles—*a dad*—to awaken me to His incredible plan for my life. I began to pray seriously about my friendship with Leslie over the following weeks. And slowly, God opened my eyes to see His fingerprints all over my relationship with this precious girl. *

I finally realized that the girl I had been praying for every

---

* *Our complete love story is detailed in our book* When Dreams Come True.

night for the past two years, the girl I had been faithfully writing love letters to, was none other than my dear friend Leslie.

And that's when another strange decision hatched.

Instead of going to Leslie with my new realization, I decided to get together with Rich.

Again the meeting took place at Perkins' Restaurant. And again, I felt incredibly awkward. I mean, how do you broach this kind of subject with a dad?

The words didn't flow as smooth and sweet as honey, but I did manage to squawk out, "Rich, I feel that God has shown me that Leslie is one day going to be my wife."

Rich had been sipping his coffee trying to wake up when I lowered that boom. It was about six a.m., and for the record, I'm sure deep and important conversations aren't supposed to take place at that time in the morning. But if Rich was having any trouble waking up, my bold statement jolted him into instant alertness.

After a moment's pause, Rich took a deep breath and spoke. Still to this day, his memorable words are some of the most cherished I've heard in my lifetime.

"Eric," he said, "Janet and I have been praying for Leslie's future husband every day since she was two years old. We prayed that we would recognize him when he came into her life. And Eric, we've known for some time now that *you are the one.*"

THE BEAUTY OF GOD-GIVEN TEAMMATES

I was hesitant to talk with Leslie about all of this. It wasn't that I was afraid of her response. In fact, as Rich and I had talked, we both felt confident that God had been showing her the same things He'd shown me about our relationship. But I was cautious about taking the "next step" with Leslie. Our friendship was so pure and Christ-centered, I worried that I might somehow mess things up by talking about a future together.

So yet another strange decision was made. Before talking with Leslie, I asked my dad and Rich if we could meet together and discuss this budding love story. I didn't want my relationship with Leslie to become just another shallow boyfriend-girlfriend romance. I wanted to build a Christ-honoring, Christ-focused relationship—radiantly pure and set apart in every aspect. Since I'd never really seen that kind of relationship modeled, I wasn't exactly sure how to go about doing it.

Through my discussions with Rich, I realized that I didn't need to figure out everything on my own. God had strategically placed teammates in my life—Leslie's parents and my parents—who could offer an outside perspective and pass along heavenly wisdom. Now, I simply needed to invite them to share in the journey.

As I sat in the Ludy family kitchen eating pizza with my dad and Rich, I asked them for guidance in how to approach this new relationship with Leslie. I figured if anyone would know the answers to my perplexing questions, it would be my God-appointed teammates. After all, they had gray hair (or in my dad's case, no hair). I was sure that they would have Gandalf-like wisdom to impart.

To my surprise, they didn't have all the answers. But they did have exactly what I really needed: support, encouragement, confirmation, and prayer.

"We aren't sure how the details are supposed to work," my dad told me. "But both Rich and I feel confident that God has put this relationship together. He will lead you if you lean on Him."

My teammates gathered around me that night, putting their strong hands on my shoulders. They prayed for this strange new love story that had begun to unfold. *They blessed my relationship with Leslie before it even began.*

At the end of the evening, Rich offered me an amazing gift. "Eric," he told me, "I give you my blessing to win my daughter's heart."

Rich handed me the key to his daughter's heart. He was opening the door for me—inviting me into Leslie's life, inviting me to pursue a future with her.

But he offered me even more than that. He offered me himself.

In the weeks and months that followed, Rich actually taught me *how* to win his daughter's heart. He trained me in the art of caring for Leslie, loving Leslie, serving Leslie, and bringing Leslie to life. We met together regularly (usually at Perkins' Restaurant!) and talked man-to-man about the art of loving a woman.

I realized on an even deeper level the amazing brilliance of God's ways. Out of all the men on Planet Earth, who knew Leslie better than her dad? My God-given teammate was the very man who was equipped to help and guide me like no other could.

Still to this day, one of my best friends in the world is a man named Rich—a dad. And to this day, Leslie sees my teammate-relationship with her father as one of the highlights of our romance. "What girl wouldn't feel like a princess," she says, "when the two most important men in her life are getting together on a regular basis to talk about nothing else but how to be sensitive to her?"

One the most rewarding aspects of our love story was our discovery of our God-given teammates—our parents. With their help, wisdom, and prayer, we experienced the breathtaking beauty of the sweeter song.

BECOMING A TEAMMATE

Leslie and I had one big advantage during the formation of our love story: we had parents who desired something more for our lives than the mediocrity of the culture.

It may sound as if our parents—especially Rich with his incredible nuggets of wisdom—had everything figured out ahead of time. It may seem as if they had a clear vision of the sweeter song from the beginning. But that wasn't the case. They were learning about the beauty of a God-scripted love story right along with us.

Like any parents, it was scary for them to see us make strange decisions—choices radically different than the culture around us. They had never seen a God-built romance take shape. It was uncharted territory for all of us. But they cheered us on as we sought to follow Christ and honor Him with our decisions.

Our parents didn't have a clear picture of exactly how they should be involved in the process of our burgeoning romance —but they were ready to be involved as God led. And as a result, they played a role in our love story that was both profound and beautiful.

As a parent, you don't need to be an expert on love and romance to make an impact on your child's future love story. *You*

> As a parent, you don't need to be an expert on love and romance to make an impact on your child's future love story. *You just need to be willing to be used by God.*

just need to be willing to be used by God. There may be times when you will stare blankly at your child's life and think, *I have no idea what to say or do in this situation!* But if you are willing to hear it, God will give you His "idea." He will work through you supernaturally. He will train you to be the ultimate teammate for your child.

Our parents were like many Christian parents today: they wanted their children to be successful in romance, but didn't quite know how to help that happen. From an early age, they taught us the things that Christianity said were important—abstinence, waiting until we were at least sixteen to date, and then dating only Christians, etc. Like us, they weren't yet familiar with something more.

But what set our parents apart from so many others was that they didn't just sit back and say, "Well, we've done all we can do. If Eric and Leslie don't turn out all right, then it's not our fault." Instead, they prayed, they studied God's Word, and they prayed some more. Our parents were willing to help us find that elusive "something better." They didn't try to make the discovery for us; they simply offered the support, encouragement, and prayer that we needed in order to find it for ourselves.

Our parents were pioneers into uncharted territories. They

didn't have a map; they only had God to lead them. But as a result of their obedience, their lives became a map for the two of us to follow. The picture of heaven-on-earth romance came more and more into focus for us, as it became more and more in focus for them.

Was it easy? No. And it won't be easy for you either. World-class parenting is rare today, because it demands a commitment that is beyond what most parents deem reasonable. It demands persistence. It demands selflessness and fierce love. But world-class parents are what the sex-at-thirteen generation needs. They need parents who are willing to be mapmakers for them, parents willing to move in directions that no one around them is moving, parents who will help their kids reach destinations other kids aren't reaching.

Catching the Vision

Unless you, as a parent, gain a vision for *something more* in your children's future marriage, you won't be able to point them in the right direction. Whether intentionally or not, you will become one of the "wet blankets" that stifles the hope that the younger generation desperately seeks.

Linda, a divorced mother of an eighteen-year-old girl, told us that she hopes her daughter will choose a career over marriage. "Men are jerks," she spat bitterly. "I don't want my daughter to get hurt like I did. She shouldn't waste her time on marriage—it just doesn't work."

You may have experienced tremendous heartbreak, abuse, abandonment, and betrayal in *your* love life. The pain may have been severe. But don't let your own pain cause you to expect similar heartache in your child's life. Rather, let your own pain fuel your desire to help them experience something *so much better.*

Self-constructed love stories always fade with time. Only God-built lives and God-written romances endure, grow, and blossom even more beautifully with time. The key to all great lives and all great love dramas is very simple, so simple that most of us walk right past it on our way down the wedding aisle. *God must be the one writing it. God must have the pen. He must be the one in control.*

The thing that makes for a great love story is the very same thing that will make you a great parent. *You must give God the pen.* You must let Him script your child's life. He must be the one in control, and you must become a servant to *His* agenda.

Today's young people need parents and leaders who model this attitude, parents and leaders who continually push them toward the beauty of a God-scripted life.

Leslie and I have found that often it is not our sex-polluted culture but *the attitude of parents* that holds the younger generation back from seeking more.

Maggie, a Christian mother of two teenagers, recently expressed to us a common parental sentiment. "Of course I want my kids to live solid Christian lives," she said, "but I don't see the need for them to become strange and isolated. I believe they can make good choices and still have a fun high school experience. I don't want them taking their convictions to an extreme. *I want them to be normal.*"

But what does "normal" mean for Christian young people today? Normal means a watered-down commitment to technical virginity. Normal means a mind polluted by the perversion of the culture. Normal means a heart trampled by one short-term fling after the next. Normal means a lackluster view of marriage. Normal means stale and mediocre love stories.

Do you really want normal for your children? Do you want them to live according to the dismal standard of our modern times? Do you want them to have only as much as you yourself have found?

Or do you want something better for them?

If you want your children to discover the depths and heights of a God-scripted love story, you must first relinquish your hold, your expectations, and your limitations on their lives. Like Abraham with his precious son Isaac in Genesis 22, you must be willing to set them on God's altar and allow *Him* to control their destiny.

For young people to uncover the beauty of a God-scripted romance, they must first give God the pen to let Him script their story. *But the same is true for you as a parent.*

It might be uncomfortable for you to see your child follow God with abandon, to walk a completely different path than the cultural norm, and to make strange decisions, like choosing to avoid short-term relationships or saving her first kiss for her wedding day. But if you allow God to inspire your child's story, it will be a story full of His grace and power, and you will never be disappointed with the outcome.

Don't hinder the younger generation from climbing to the glorious heights that God has for them. Your attitude is crucial. Begin cheering them on toward lives of complete abandonment and surrender to Jesus Christ. No, they will never be normal. But they will discover the most fulfilling life of all.

MAKING IT PRACTICAL

> ### True-Love Challenge #1
> Your personal past is causing you to limit your child's future.
>
> ### The True-Love Answer
> Move past your past to serve your child's future love story.

Your past is real. It happened. But today is a day for new beginnings. Today represents a fresh opportunity to ask God to remake your life and shape you into a living demonstration of His victorious life. Today represents a fresh opportunity to see Him take all your mistakes and transform them into little pieces of purposeful hope for the future. You don't have to be perfect to serve your child's future, just willing and ready. You don't have to be perfect to be remade by Jesus Christ, just willing to be made perfect more and more throughout your life.

If you have experienced pain in your own life, let it motivate you to help your child discover something better. But don't resign yourself to defeat. The same God who can write a beautiful love story for your child is the same God who wants to take the pen of your life and script for you an amazing life story for you from this day forward. God didn't come to this earth to save the perfect; He came for you and me—the messed up and seriously in need of help. Let Him wash you clean and set you on the right course afresh this very day. It is never too late to turn and walk a new way.

ACTION PLAN

Three Practical Ways to Tackle This Challenge
In Your Life Today

1. **Seek a heavenly springtime for your soul.** Spring is a time for new beginnings; it's a time for new life and new attitudes. Allow God to take you through a time of spiritual renewal and refreshment. Schedule some time alone with God, allowing Him to restore your soul. Whether you sneak away for an hour, a weekend, or longer, the important thing is to quiet your mind, remove all distractions, and spend time in His presence, gaining His perspective on your past and your future. Ask God for a new beginning; He loves to give them. If you find that you are dealing with unresolved hurt, bitterness, or inner turmoil over your past, consider working with a Biblical counselor or godly mentor for a period of time. Their prayers, encouragement, and support may go a long way toward helping you embrace a fresh new season in your life.

2. **Turn on the light of truth.** Let God's light shine within your life. Let Him point out things that you may be hiding in the deep shadows of your soul—secrets that need to be dealt with. When spring comes, it's time for spring cleaning. Allow God to gently begin the trash removal process. Allow Him to blow His fresh clean scent into your inner life. (For some extra

guidance in this process, please visit www.whengodwrites.com and look at the inner sanctuary material provided there.)

3. Right your wrongs. When God's light shines, He often puts His finger on specific people we have wronged, and He nudges us to make those wrongs right. As you begin the process of encouraging your child toward healthy relationships, be willing to begin the very same process in your own life, even if it means getting uncomfortable. (More on this process can be found in the inner sanctuary material on www.whengodwrites.com.)

MAKING IT PRACTICAL

True-Love Challenge #2
It's easy to become cynical about God's ability to script beautiful love stories.

The True-Love Answer
Allow God to be as big as He says He is in your child's love life.

For many people, life has been marred by pain and disappointment. The dreams of happiness and love they once cherished have eroded over time into one gigantic nightmare. Many of us dreamed big as little kids, but we no longer allow ourselves to dream as adults. We don't believe life can offer anything better than what we have already experienced. We hide behind cynicism to protect ourselves from more disappointment.

When God delivered the Israelites out of Egypt, he gave them a promise of a land flowing with milk and honey. He gave them a vision of something more. Many of them believed Him in the beginning. They put the blood of the lamb on their doorposts and God delivered them out of Egypt, even parting the Red Sea so they could cross over. They saw the miraculous. They experienced the power of their God.

But then they entered the desert.

The desert was hot, miserable, and difficult. They began to wilt beneath the misery, longing for the land of Canaan but doubting that God really meant what He said. Maybe this wilderness life was all He ever intended to give them, they thought.

But God hadn't lied to them. He wanted them to follow Him into the beautiful land. Yet the Israelites no longer believed God could do what He said He could do. They became cynics, and an entire generation of them died in the desert (See Joshua 5:6; Psalm 106:21–27).

Yes, the desert is hot and miserable. But God allows us to feel the heat of the wilderness so that we long to move on, so that we ask Him to take us further. Leave the cynic behind, and press on into the fullness of what God originally called you to discover.

ACTION PLAN

Three Practical Ways to Tackle This Challenge
In Your Life Today

1. Weigh yourself on the cynic scale. Are you a doubter or a firm believer in God's ability to work the impossible? Do you believe that the culture's agenda for your child's life is more powerful than God's ability to build your child's life into a triumphant display of His love and truth? If you find that you're lugging around some heavy cynicism, then begin a steady new diet, chewing on His promises for an abundant life. Allowing God to prove His faithfulness is the surest and most effective way to take off the cynic weight.

2. Take some time to meditate on the promises of God. Allow your mind to be transformed by a heavenly perspective. Catch a vision for God's faithfulness and purpose in your own life and in the life of your child. Some great promises to start with are Jeremiah 29:11, Isaiah 40:31, Psalm 91, John 14:16–21, and Philippians 4:6–7. For an extra boost of encouragement in everyday life, copy down your favorite God-promises and put them in a place where you will see them often, such as on your bathroom mirror or in your wallet. Train your mind to habitually dwell on His truth, and soon your entire attitude and outlook will be transformed.

3. Start a spiritual journal. Set aside time each day or each week to write down prayers, hopes, and dreams for both your life and your child's life. Anytime you observe God's hand at work, even in small ways, write it down in your journal. As time passes, periodically read back over your prayer requests and spiritual observations, and soon you will begin to notice a clear, unmistakable pattern of God's loving faithfulness in your life.

MAKING IT PRACTICAL

True-Love Challenge #3
It's tempting to try to script your child's life and love story according to your own agenda.

The True-Love Answer
Relinquish the pen to the Author of the truest love and life success.

The beautiful things God has in store for us are never found in the desert of our own self-effort. We can try and try to create a great life for ourselves and for our children, but it's simply impossible to discover heavenly things through human means.

God needs to take over. He knows your desire to see your child enter the beautiful land. Let Him have the control. Let Him have that precious child of yours to do with as He sees fit, no matter what that means. When God takes over a life, He may allow that person to be imprisoned, tortured, or even martyred for His glory. He may ask your child to be single or to patiently wait for many long, uncomfortable years before finding a beautiful love story. But only when God takes over a child's life can he or she discover heaven on earth.

Adoniram Judson, pioneer missionary to India, wrote this

statement in a letter to his future bride's parents when asking for her hand in marriage: "I have now to ask whether you can consent to part with your daughter . . . consent to her departure to a heathen land and her subjection to the hardships and sufferings of a missionary life. To consent to her exposure to every kind of want and distress, to degradation, insult, persecution, and perhaps a violent death. Can you consent to all this for the sake of Him who died for her and for you?"[1]

As parents, you must ask yourself the same question. Are you willing to give your children back to the One who gave everything for you?

God is the only One who is capable of scripting lifelong love stories and truly fulfilling *life* stories—so let Him have the pen of your child's life and love story. And while you're at it, give Him the pen to script your own life and love story. You'll never regret one moment lived while possessed by the Spirit of Almighty God.

ACTION PLAN

Three Practical Ways to Tackle This Challenge
In Your Life Today

1. Make a commitment to give God the pen. Steal away to a quiet place where you won't be distracted. Calm your mind, quiet your heart, and then consciously surrender your agenda and expectations to the God of the universe. It doesn't have to be a complicated prayer, just a few simple words telling God that you are ready to let Him have His way. You may find it beneficial to put your commitment in writing. Whenever you find yourself trying to take the pen back and script your own story, take a moment to reread your commitment and re-submit the situation to the One who loves you more than you can possibly know.

2. Gain a vision for true surrender. For a poignant example of what surrender to God really means, read Genesis 22, the story of Abraham's willingness to sacrifice his only son, Isaac. Then, read about the greatest surrender to God that ever was, in Philippians 2:5–11 and Matthew 26:39. Allow these stories to be a constant reminder of the life we are called to as Christ-followers—a life fully submitted to the King of all kings.

3. Identify areas of weakness. Take time each day or week to allow God to search your heart and bring to light any specific situation in which you are still clinging to your own agenda. On a regular basis, ask Him to show you any area in your life or your child's life that you are trying to humanly manipulate. Then, make a conscious decision to let go of the pen and let God have His way in that area. It is difficult to let go of the control, but as you see God's faithfulness time and time again, you will wonder why you ever doubted Him.

MAKING IT PRACTICAL

> ### True-Love Challenge #4
> You aren't sure how to offer the true-love guidance and support your child needs.
>
> ### The True-Love Answer
> Help your child find true-love success by joining his or her team.

God-written love stories don't happen when parents are the ones in control of a child's love life. They happen only when *God* is the One in control of your child's love life. Don't try to write your child's love story. Instead, point your son or daughter to the One who is capable of writing the most amazing stories of all—God Himself. Teach your child to pursue a God-scripted life. And as your child navigates the journey, don't neglect your vital God-given role in the process. Remember that God has anointed and commissioned you to protect and provide for your child—spiritually, emotionally, and physically. Be his cheerleader as he seeks a set-apart life. Provide him with practical help and wisdom as God guides you. Be available to listen to his struggles and desires. Be willing to speak boldly when necessary. And be willing to let your child take steps forward when God leads.

One of the most commonly asked questions we receive from young people is, "How will I know when God is initiating a romantic relationship in my life?" Godly parents can serve as a wonderful source of guidance as a young person seeks God's direction in this area. Parents who are tuned in to God are blessed with special spiritual insight into their children's lives. As a godly teammate, you are meant to serve as rear-view and side-view mirrors for your child to consult when it's time to make a lane change. Godly teammates are equipped to offer a heavenly perspective—to provide confirmation of a God-initiated relationship, or to offer caution when caution is needed.

In order to fulfill this God-given role, you must not lean on your own wisdom or be propelled by your own agenda. Instead, spend time on your knees, diligently praying and seeking God's wisdom for your child. Allow Him to lead and guide you. Allow Him to be the One in control. Allow Him to work through you as you become a godly teammate in your child's life, and you will discover the amazing depth and reach of parenting.

ACTION PLAN

Three Practical Ways to Tackle This Challenge in Your Life Today

1. Join forces with your spouse. As a couple, take time to formulate a specific vision for how you want to be involved in your child's future love story. Discuss practical ways you can become joint teammates for your son or daughter through prayer, counsel, and God-directed involvement in his or her romantic life. Put your unified vision in writing and commit it to God. When relational situations and questions arise, take some time together to prayerfully consider how God wants you to respond. If you are single or in a marriage situation in which a joint effort isn't possible, then take some time alone with God and allow Him to give you a specific vision of your teammate role in your child's life. Put your vision in writing and commit it to God. Even if you are a solo teammate, always remember that you have an undefeated Coach. If you lean on His guidance, He will never let you down.

2. Facilitate a teammate discussion with your child. Take time to sit with your child and express your vision for being a teammate in this area of her life. Share specific ways you want to help discover God's very best for your child's future love life. Let her know how you are going to be praying. Share your vision for the teammate relationship you want to have with her. Remember, you can't force yourself onto a young person's team, you must be invited. Open up a discussion, allowing her to share her own desires and thoughts. And don't make it a one-time conversation. Be sure to keep yourself 100 percent available anytime she needs you.

3. Make a standing date with your child. Once a month (or more often if you desire), take your child out for a special afternoon or evening. Whether you go to a nice dinner or for simple a walk in the park, the important thing is to remove all distractions and simply focus on being together. Don't use this time for lectures, corrections, or logistical discussions. Rather, ask deep questions about what's really going on inside your child—his thoughts, dreams, struggles, and walk with God. Take time to really listen and understand what he is going through. As he senses your genuine desire to know him, he will begin to open up to you more and more. As you make your child a true priority, you will open the door for an amazing teammate relationship in every area of his life.

In a Nutshell

The key to every great life and every great love drama is very simple: *God must be the one writing it. God must have the pen. He must be the one in control.*

And the thing that makes for a great love story is the very same thing that will make you a great parent: *You must give him the pen.* You must let Him script your child's life. He must be the one in control, and you must become a servant to *His* agenda.

Leslie and I had one big advantage during the formation of our love story—we had God-given teammates. We had parents who desired something more for our lives than the mediocrity of the culture. They were willing to allow God to hold the pen throughout the entire drama.

Our parents didn't have a clear picture of exactly how they should be involved in the process of our burgeoning romance, but they were ready to be involved as God led. And as a result, they played a role in our love story that was both profound and beautiful.

As a parent, you don't need to be an expert on love and romance to make an impact on your child's future love story. *You just need to be willing to be used by God.* There may be times when you will stare blankly at your child's life and think, *I have no idea what to say or do in this situation!* But if you are willing to hear it, God will give you His "idea." He will work through you supernaturally. He will train you to be the ultimate teammate for your child.

Part Two

A GOD-WRITTEN LOVE STORY

Unless the LORD builds the house, they labor in vain who build it.
—PSALM 127:1 NASB

Trust in the LORD with all your heart and do not lean on your own understanding.
—PROVERBS 3:5 NASB

I have been crucified with Christ; and it is no longer I who live, but Christ lives in me.
—GALATIANS 2:20 NASB

It must not be what I want, but what you want.
—MATTHEW 26:39 PHILLIPS

3

THE FUEL OF A GOD-WRITTEN LOVE STORY

*Helping kids unlock the secret
to a successful romance*

Leslie

WHAT REALLY MATTERS

EVERY MONTH, ERIC AND I receive hundreds of relationship questions from young people. "Should I pursue this relationship?" "Should I stay in this relationship?" "How can I keep Christ at the center of my relationship?" "How will I know when to take the next step in this relationship?" The list goes on and on.

These young people desire to build a relationship the right way. They want to find something beautiful, something that can stand the test of time. They want to make the right decisions in this crucial area of their lives. In their own way, they are all asking the same universal question: *how do I do this right?*

It's easy to come up with human-constructed answers to that all-important question. From superstrict rules to vague moral boundaries, the Christian community is brimming with theories and solutions about how to help kids discover God's best in relationships.

A woman wrote to us with an interesting theory. "I think that we should keep boys and girls completely separated until they are twenty-one," she declared. "And when they are ready for marriage, I think their parents should arrange the match."

A father of four offered a different approach. "I think that as long as you keep your kids surrounded by Christian peers and protect them from negative influences like raunchy movies and Internet porn, for the most part they'll end up making good choices."

But building a successful relationship doesn't come from a complicated formula or a set of moral guidelines. True relational success all comes down to one simple question: *who holds the pen of your life?*

> When God is at the center of a relationship, young people naturally make the right choices because they are listening to *His* voice rather than the voice of their own selfish desires.

When young people script their own stories, no amount of Christian guidelines or moral advice can help them experience the matchless beauty of heaven-built love. As parents and leaders, we often focus on the surface issues of relational success. We ask young people questions such as, "Are you saving sex until marriage?" "Are you dating only Christians?"

But when God holds the pen of their lives, when God scripts their story, those questions don't even need to be asked. When God is at the center of a relationship, young people naturally make the right choices because they are listening to *His* voice rather than the voice of their own selfish desires.

A God-centered existence is the only fuel for a truly successful romance. Until that foundation is in place, young people will always flounder and struggle in relationship building. It's tempting to come up with human strategies and guidelines. But as true-love teammates for the younger generation, it's time we start offering them the key to true success—*a God-scripted love story.*

In the previous chapter, we talked about the importance of allowing God to hold the pen and script a young person's love story. Now, let's take a deeper look at what a God-scripted story really looks like.

Modern young people, as well as parents, often have misconceptions about what it really means to build a God-centered romance. Eric and I continually encounter young adults who desire the beauty and benefits of a God-written love story yet still want to maintain control over their own pen.

Holly is a college freshman who sought our advice on her current dating relationship. "My boyfriend is a great Christian guy," she told me. "But our relationship isn't built around Christ. We tend to focus on each other and tune God out. And we always find ourselves doing things physically that we regret. I know we're off track, but I don't want to give up what I have with this guy. Is there a way I can stay in this relationship and still be close to God?"

Holly represents a generation of Christian young people who are well practiced in doing the bare minimum for God. They want to "have their cake and eat it too"—to maintain their own agenda yet still gain the fulfillment of a God-scripted story.

But when God holds the pen, He requests everything we are. He asks us to give Him complete control over every aspect of our lives. He calls us to build our lives completely around Him, to jealously guard our relationship with Him, and to keep Him at the center of our existence, including our love life.

If Holly were truly experiencing a God-scripted love story, the relationship would look very different. Being with her boyfriend would not draw her away from God but closer and closer to Him. She wouldn't be clinging to the relationship; she would be holding it with an open hand, allowing God to have His way. She and her boyfriend wouldn't be indulging themselves in selfish physical gratification; they would be constantly seeking to honor God and each other every moment they were together. If ever she realized the relationship was not glorifying Him, she would walk away from it. She would allow nothing, not even a cherished relationship, to stand in the way of her obedience to her Lord.

Many young people think when they find a "great Christian guy" or "a godly young woman" that God must have brought them together. But a God-scripted story isn't two Christians coming together in a human-constructed relationship. Rather, it is two lives fully surrendered to Jesus Christ, building each aspect of their relationship under the gentle guidance and direction of God's Spirit.

Giving God the pen isn't merely deciding that we want the benefits of a God-scripted love story. It is a crucial decision of the will—the choice to lay down our own agenda and let Christ overtake our being and live His life through us.

When I was sixteen, I was struggling intensely with making this decision. I had always thought that I could somehow appease God by living a basically moral life. Inwardly, I hoped that He would stay out of the way and let me make my own decisions when it came to romance. As long as I could be the one in control, calling the shots, deciding who to go out with and who to marry, then I didn't mind following a few Christian guidelines along the way.

But God began to softly knock on the door of my heart, challenging me to turn my life's pen over to Him. It was around that time that I read the story of Dr. Walter Wilson, a Christian physician in the early 1900s who made the decision to surrender his entire life to the God of the universe. His prayer of absolute abandonment shook me to the core.

> "Lord, I give You this body of mine; from my head to my feet, I give it to You." He prayed, "My hands, my limbs, my eyes, my brain; all that I am inside and out, I hand over to You. Live in and through me whatever life You please. You may send this body to Africa, or lay it on bed with cancer. You may blind my eyes, or send me with Your message to Tibet. You may take this body to the Eskimos, or send it to a hospital with pneumonia. This body of mind is Yours alone from this moment on."[1]

When I read that prayer, I knew what God was asking of me. And I knew that I was finally ready to let Him overtake my being. Kneeling beside my bed one morning, I laid my soul bare before God as Walter Wilson had done.

"Lord, I give you this body of mine," I prayed. "Live in and through me whatever life You please. I give You my love life. You can keep me single for the rest of my life. You can match me with whomever You see fit. I lay down my own agenda and my own dreams. I give up all control. Take the pen. Write my love story—and my life story—in Your own time, in Your own way."

I rose from my knees, an incredible peace and freedom flooding my soul. It was at that moment that my life truly began. It was at that moment when I finally understood the foundation for true love—complete surrender to the Author of romance Himself.

It was this foundation alone that allowed Eric and me to experience the fullness of a God-scripted story. Unless young people yield their entire existence to the God of the universe, they will never be able to build anything more than a self-constructed human love story with a "Christian" label stuck on it.

WAITING ON GOD

Just as I was terrified to give God the pen of my life at the age of sixteen, parents often experience the same fear when it comes to giving their children to God. They don't want to see their kids placing "unrealistic" expectations upon God, only to be disappointed in the end.

"God can't steer a parked car," spouted a youth pastor during a discussion on romance. "I tell the kids in my group that God doesn't want us wandering around helplessly, waiting on Him for every decision. It's up to them to choose who to date and who to marry. God will bless their decisions if they live a moral life."

"Waiting on God is all well and good," declared a mother of two teens. "But I don't want my kids to miss out on life. I tell them to get out there and meet people, to date around and decide what type of person they are compatible with. God helps those who help themselves!"

Many Christian parents have acknowledged Christ as their Savior and built their life around Christian guidelines yet never actually yielded their entire existence to the God of the universe. They have never allowed Him to take over their existence and live His life through them. They have never experienced what Paul was referring to when he said, "I no longer live, but Christ lives in me" (Galatians 2:20). And as a result they encourage their kids toward a moral, self-built lifestyle rather than a radically surrendered, God-scripted life.

But encouraging our kids to give God the pen does not create unrealistic expectations. The Author of romance is eager and waiting to write an amazing love story for our children. He cares even more about this area of their lives than you do as a parent. He doesn't just want to stand at a distance and offer His general blessing on our kids' lives and decisions. He wants to be intimately involved in every detail.

As humans we are naturally drawn to statements such as "God helps those who help themselves." We like being in control. We'd rather follow a set of moral guidelines and ask for God's blessing than fully yield our entire lives to His leading and direction.

But a fully yielded life is exactly what He wants for us and for our children.

When Christ lived on this earth, He gave us the ultimate example of complete surrender to the God of the universe. He did nothing of His own accord (see John 14:10). His constant prayer to His Father was, "Not my will, but yours be done" (Luke 22:42). As He went about His ministry, He constantly listened and yielded to the voice of His Father.

That's what it means to give God the pen and let Him script our story. It means having the very attitude of Christ, constantly saying to God, "Not my will, but yours be done."

Waiting on God and allowing Him to guide us is not a

passive process. When Eric and I encourage young people to wait on God, we don't mean they should sit in their room twenty-four hours a day, afraid to go anywhere or do anything until they hear a booming voice from heaven.

Waiting on God is an *active* process, just as waiting on tables in a restaurant is an active job. A waiter in a restaurant must be continually aware of his patrons' needs, continually seeking to serve and please the customer. Waiting on God is similar. It's a daily pursuit of Him. It means seeking Him continually, communicating with Him hourly, and listening to His gentle whisper on a moment-to-moment basis. It means allowing His Spirit to hold us back or nudge us forward as He desires.

Charles Trumbull said it this way: "Jesus Christ does not want to be our helper; He wants to be our Life. He does not want us to work for Him. He wants us to let Him do His work through us, using us as we use a pencil to write with."[2]

KEEPING GOD AT THE CENTER

Experiencing a God-scripted story may sound distant and complicated. But in reality, it is dazzlingly simple. Once we give God the pen of our existence, we no longer have to control or manipulate circumstances. We no longer have to go through the exhausting process of trying to figure everything out on our own. Our only job is to lean, to yield, to trust, and to obey. God does the rest. In Matthew 6, Jesus gave the formula for true success in every area of life: seek first His kingdom—His rulership over your life—and everything else will fall into place (see verse 33).

So how does that lead to a God-scripted love story?

A young man named Blane recently asked me, "How did

you know that God was leading you into a relationship with Eric? Did He give you a special revelation? Did you hear an audible voice from heaven?"

The process of letting God lead my love story with Eric was far less extreme than Blane was imagining. God didn't send mystical signs from Heaven or angels to visit me in the night. Rather, as I built my life around Him and sought His guidance, He gently awakened my heart to His plan. As I waited on Him and yielded to Him, He faithfully opened all the right doors. I didn't have to manipulate any part of my relationship with Eric. As I listened to the voice of God, He cautioned me where caution was needed. And He nudged me forward when it was time to take the next step.

When Eric and I knew that our friendship was headed toward a future together, we surrendered our relationship back to God. "Lord, we give You our emotions, our desires, and our expectations," Eric prayed as we sat on a grassy hill one summer afternoon. "We don't want to be the ones leading this relationship. We want You to build it from start to finish. May we wait for Your direction and not rush ahead with our own agenda."

Whenever Eric and I spent time together, we began by praying that God's presence would be with us. Whenever we needed to make a decision about our relationship, we spent time individually seeking God. We each continued to guard our individual relationships with Christ as our highest priority, rather than allowing our relationship with each other to become our central focus. We continually asked Him to search our hearts and show us if there was any area in which we had taken the pen back out of His hands.

As we yielded to Him in this way, He wrote our story.

Whenever we began to veer off track, even in small ways, He gently pricked our hearts and steered us back to Himself. When we felt it was time to take the next step in our relationship and become engaged, we waited until He filled our hearts with His perfect peace and confirmed His direction in unmistakable ways.

Keeping God at the center of our relationship wasn't a long, laborious process. It wasn't a magic formula we followed. It was the simple act of fully yielding to our God.

Our story is certainly not the only one of its kind. Every year, Eric and I receive wedding invitations from all over the country. They come from young people who entrusted the pen of their life to God and watched the Author of romance faithfully script their love story.

"I never knew how amazing my love story could be until I gave God control of this area of my life," they tell us. "It was so much more fulfilling and beautiful than anything I could have dreamed for myself!"

God-written love stories have been around since the beginning of time. They are marked by lives that submit to His faithful leading.

When Abraham's servant went out to seek a wife for Isaac, he trusted the Author of true love as his guide. He prayed that God would send the right young woman to the drinking well where he sat, and before his prayer was even complete, Rebekah appeared with a watering jar on her shoulder. When the servant learned who she was, he knew God had answered his prayer for guidance, that this was His chosen wife for Isaac.

"I bowed down and worshiped the LORD," said the servant, "for He led me on the right road to the granddaughter of my master's brother (Genesis 24:48)."

When Ruth was widowed and alone, she chose to trust God for a husband, rather than take matters into her own hands. He faithfully guided her to Boaz and gave her favor in his eyes. "You have not run after the younger men, whether rich or poor," Boaz praised her. "May the Lord bless you" (Ruth 3:10).

When the carpenter Joseph was struggling with the decision of whether he should marry a young girl who had become pregnant, God directed his steps. "Do not be afraid to take Mary home as your wife," was the clear message Joseph received from heaven, "because what is conceived in her is from the Holy Spirit" (Matthew 1:20). God had chosen Joseph to share with Mary in the sacred task of bringing up the Savior of the world. He led them together in a supernatural display of His faithfulness.

Since the creation of Adam and Eve, God has been in the business of writing beautiful, lifelong love stories. When we encourage today's young people to entrust their lives to the Author of love, they will never be disappointed. He is the most faithful Matchmaker of all.

MAKING IT PRACTICAL

True-Love Challenge #5
You want to help your child catch the vision for a God-written love story.

The True-Love Answer
Introduce your child to the Author of romance.

As parents and leaders, our role is to introduce our children to the Author of romance so that they can give their pen to Him. We can't make the decision for them, but we *can* awaken them to the matchless beauty of a God-scripted life.

The opportunities begin at an early age.

A father of a ten-year-old girl told us that he constantly looks for ways to shape his daughter's vision for the future. Instead of making comments such as, "One day when you start going out with boys . . ." he says things like, "One day, when God brings your future husband into your life . . ." He tells his daughter that God has an amazing plan for her future love story. As a result, his daughter has a different perspective on her future romance than most other girls her age. She doesn't picture herself turning sixteen and flitting from one boy to the next. She plans on waiting for God to bring a Christlike man into her life in His own time and way.

A mother of an eight-year-old boy said that she is training her son how to let God direct and lead him, even at his young age. "My son accepted Christ when he was six," she told us. "But I don't want him to only know Christ as his Savior. I want him to know Christ as the Lord of his life. It's never too early to teach him how to listen to God's voice and obey." She recognizes that as she trains her son to surrender each area of his life to his God, she is helping him gain the foundation for a God-scripted future.

When we help kids cultivate their own individual, intimate relationships with Christ, they will learn what it means to let Him take control. We must not merely give today's kids head-knowledge about Christ. We must teach them how to pursue Him, worship Him, and listen to His voice. We must show them how to submit themselves to His leading and entrust their pen into His faithful hands.

If your child is already past those early malleable years, you can still help point him or her toward a God-written life, starting today. A mother of a fifteen-year-old girl told us that she recently sat down with her daughter and admitted that she'd failed to communicate God's perspective on romance and relationships. "I know that I've never expected more for you than the typical dating scene," she told her daughter. "But now I realize that God has something so much better for your future. I want to encourage you to wait for Him to script your love story and not settle for anything less."

You might feel that your words fall upon deaf ears. But continue to plant seeds in their lives by speaking the truth. Continue to be an example to your children by giving God the pen of *your* life. And most importantly, continue to utilize your most powerful weapon of all: prayer.

Early in my teen years, I was anything but yielded to God. I was making destructive choices. I was on the path to sabotaging my future. Because I had distanced myself from my parents, they felt helpless in knowing how to reach me. But they continued to diligently and faithfully pray that God would turn my life around. He answered their prayers beyond anything they ever hoped. Don't give up on your child. You serve a God who loves and cares for them even more than you do.

ACTION PLAN

*Three Practical Ways to Tackle This Challenge
in Your Life Today*

1. **Read vision-forming books together.** If your child is
willing, schedule time with him or her to read books that paint
a vision of a God-scripted love story. (Some book suggestions:
*When God Writes Your Love Story, When Dreams Come True,
Authentic Beauty* (for girls), *God's Gift to Women* (for guys), and
Elisabeth Elliot's books *Passion and Purity* and *Quest for Love.* A
great way to do this is to go through one chapter each week and
take time to discuss it together. Eric and I recently met a single
father who had begun going through these books with his
college-aged daughter. Their times of reading and talking were
not only facilitating godly decisions in his daughter's life, but
they also inspired him to make commitments in this area of his
own life. Father and daughter are now accountability partners
and teammates for each other as they both pursue a set-apart
life. Every night, they spend a few minutes talking about their
day, sharing any struggles, victories, or prayer requests, and
taking time to lift each other up in prayer.

2. **Help your child build his or her life around Christ.**
When your child is still in the formative years, it's essential to
teach her how to make time alone with Christ her highest daily
priority. Parents often plan their children's days to include a
plethora of "important" things such as school, sports, music,
and social activities, but fail to schedule in time for the most
important thing of all—their relationship with God. When my
brothers were about eight and ten, my parents began to carve

out time in their morning schedule for them to be alone with God. They were encouraged to study their Bible, write in their journal, pray, or sing worship songs. My parents exhorted them to utilize this quiet time to seek God and listen to His voice. Before long those quiet times became extremely important to my brothers. Even at their young age, their time alone with God each morning gave them a spiritual foundation that carried them through the rest of their day.

If your child is past the early years but is open to making Christ a true priority in his or her daily life, you can still assist in this goal. Encourage your daughter to evaluate how she spends her time each day. Help your son identify pastimes or activities that might be distracting him from time with Christ. It's easy to make young people feel that they need to be constantly "going and doing" in order to be normal and healthy, but the best thing we can encourage them to do is build their daily life around time with Jesus Christ—even if they don't accomplish as much. You may have to encourage your children to make tough decisions, such as cutting out certain activities or pursuits, in order to build their day around time with God. But be bold enough to give them a verbal and practical push toward making Christ their first priority.

MAKING IT PRACTICAL

True-Love Challenge #6
The culture is out to sabotage God's true-love
intention for your child's life.

The True-Love Answer
Become a champion for the set-apart lifestyle.

As our kids grow into young adults, we must continue to point them toward a God-written existence. Without realizing it, many parents and leaders pressure young people to follow the trends of the culture rather than the voice of God.

"So, do you have a boyfriend, Leslie?" was the constant query I received from youth leaders, relatives, and my parents' friends growing up. It seems like a harmless question to ask a young person. But it only reinforced the idea that I wasn't a "normal and healthy" teenager unless I was jumping from one short-term relationship to the next. Through innocent comments from well-meaning adults, I was constantly tempted to take matters into my own hands instead of waiting for God to script my love story in His own time and way.

The modern Christian culture does not often provide much support for young people who have chosen to give God the pen of their love life. Lyndie, a high school sophomore, echoed this frustration to me in a recent e-mail. "The Christians in my life are always asking me, 'What's going on in your love life?' They never ask, 'What's going on in your relationship with Jesus Christ?'"

Michael, a college freshman, has chosen to wait for God's leading before he pursues a romantic relationship. "Other Christians make me feel like a freak for living this way," he told us. "When I told a Christian friend that I had decided not to date around, he just looked at me funny and then asked if I was gay."

As parents and leaders, we can have a tremendous impact upon the younger generation's decision to give God the pen of their lives. It may seem easier to win the favor of the younger crowd by asking them who they are dating or what's happening in their love life. But those questions only convey that we expect nothing more for them than a human-built, mediocre love story.

Let's begin asking the younger generation the *right* questions. A youth pastor named Dave told us that his focus is not to entertain and coddle the kids in his ministry, but to continually challenge them toward the standard of Jesus Christ. And sometimes this takes him out of his comfort zone.

"It's hard to confront a young person and ask where God is in his or her life," Dave told us. "It's difficult to challenge a young dating couple to evaluate whether God is truly at the center of their life and relationship. But those are the questions they need to hear. Kids don't just need a buddy. They need an example of Christ."

Eric and I couldn't agree more. The longer we work with the younger generation, the more we realize how much they need Christian parents and leaders to challenge them to surrender their existence to the King of all kings.

We will see amazing things happen in the younger generation when parents and leaders finally begin to *expect* kids to pursue a God-written love story rather than the culture's version of romance.

ACTION PLAN

Two Practical Ways to Tackle This Challenge
in Your Life Today

1. **Brainstorm questions to ask your child on a regular basis.** Take some time to think and pray about certain questions that you can ask your child. Write down a list of the questions that come to mind, and then begin looking for opportunities to voice them. Ask questions such as, "How has God been working in your life?" or, "How have you been challenged in your commitment to living a set-apart life?" At first this might seem awkward and uncomfortable, but asking challenging questions can go a long way in helping your child keep focused on what truly matters. Be sure to express yourself in a loving, genuine way rather than in a stern tone of inquisition. And as you discuss spiritual things with your child, don't make it a one-way street. Share what God has been teaching you and showing you in your own spiritual journey, and you will set an inspiring example for your child to follow.

2. **Evaluate the influences in your child's life.** In our modern culture, we often allow certain influences into our child's life because it is the "normal" thing to do. We want our kids to be well-rounded and healthy, and we often assume that means they need to have a certain number of friends and participate in certain activities. When it comes to influences such as TV, the

Internet, movies, books, friends, sports, and social activities, the line of "harmful vs. helpful" often appears blurry. But here is a great litmus test: If any pastime, friendship, activity, or influence is distracting your child from Christ and leading him further away from God's perspective, then it does not belong in his life.

Take some time to examine the spiritual fruit that is being produced in your child's life as a result of each influence, friendship, or activity he is exposed to. Is your child becoming more hardened to the things of God, more like the culture around him, more consumed with temporal, material things, or less interested in his walk with Christ? If so, be willing to do whatever it takes to protect your child from the things that are pulling him in the wrong direction, even if you fear that he will "miss out" on something important. In reality, the only thing he will be missing is a compromised and spiritually dead existence.

A PICTURE OF GOD-WRITTEN ROMANCE

Wheaton, Illinois
1947

On a chilly winter day in 1947, a young college girl named Elisabeth sat in the school auditorium listening to a passionate speaker. "Do not stir up or awaken love," the speaker exhorted his audience, "until God initiates the relationship." Elisabeth's heart was pricked by the challenging words. Many of her college friends had already found serious relationships. Some were engaged or married. Elisabeth felt called to a life of service for God, but she couldn't seem to ignore the longing in her heart for an earthly love story.

God was asking Elisabeth to surrender that desire to Him; to give Him the pen of her life and allow Him to script her story . . . even if it meant a life of singleness. Could she trust Him that much?

"God was sifting me," Elisabeth wrote later. "What kind of a God is it who asks everything of us? The same God who did not spare his own Son, but gave Him up for us all. He gives all. He asks all."

Elisabeth gave all to Him. She surrendered her longing for marriage. "I wanted to be loved," Elisabeth said. "But I [also] wanted something deeper." The "something deeper" she wanted was a Christ-ruled, Christ-centered existence. And He was asking for total control. "Lord," she prayed, "here's my heart."

Living out her commitment became even more challenging when she met a fiery young Christian named Jim Elliot. The more she got to know Jim, the more she saw that he was the picture of everything she hoped for in a husband. "He was a real man," she said, "strong, friendly, and handsome. He loved God. That was the supreme dynamic of his life. Nothing else mattered much by comparison."

Soon Jim began to show an interest in her. But God continued to challenge her to surrender the friendship back to Him—not to cling to the hope of a relationship but to leave the pen in His hands. Elisabeth struggled deeply with the challenge. "A settled commitment to the Lord Christ and a longed-for commitment to Jim Elliot seemed to be in conflict," she wrote. "I was only a college girl, trying to do well in my studies, praying for direction for my life, attracted to a very appealing man whose primary interest was in the Kingdom of God. [What was] wrong with that?"

But God wanted everything, even the "good" desires of her heart.

One day Jim told Elisabeth that he was in love with her. The revelation was bittersweet. Elisabeth's heart soared at Jim's words, but became sober again when he went on to say that God had challenged him to embrace a life of singleness—perhaps for life, or perhaps only for a season.

"I've given you and all my feelings for you to God," Jim said. "He'll have to work out whatever He wants. If I marry, I know who it will be. I want you. But you're not mine." Jim spoke of the story of Abraham's offering up of the most precious thing in his life: his son Isaac. "So I put you on the altar," he told her.

Elisabeth and Jim agreed to pray steadily about their future and wait patiently until God made the way plain. Waiting was excruciatingly difficult. "Is God interested in the plight of two college kids?" Elisabeth wondered. "Has our cause perhaps escaped His notice? Will He bother with us, when He is busy with who knows how many worlds?"

Elisabeth and Jim believed God wanted to be involved in the intimate details of their lives and decisions. So they continued to trust. They continued to wait. No matter how strong their feelings were, they would not rush ahead of Him.

"A good and perfect gift, these natural desires," wrote Elisabeth later. "But so much more the necessity that they be restrained, controlled, even crucified, that they might be reborn in power and purity for God. For us, this was the way we had to walk, and we walked it. Jim seeing it his duty to protect me, I seeing it mine to wait quietly, not to attempt to woo or entice."

Elisabeth and Jim didn't just wait on God for a week. They didn't just wait a month. They didn't just wait for a year. Five years passed while the two young people sought God's direction. They remained committed to each other, but they were careful to guard their emotions and pursue nothing more than a Christ-centered friendship until God showed them otherwise. The road was narrow and lonely. But Elisabeth and Jim understood the difference between self-focused human love and a love scripted by the God of creation.

"A man's love for a woman ought to hold her to the highest," Elisabeth said. "Her love for him ought to do the same. I did not want to turn Jim aside from the call of God, to distract his energies, or in any way to stand between him and surrender. This was what I understood real love to mean. Purity comes at a high price. Sometimes the sacrifice makes little sense to others, but when offered to God it is always accepted."

Finally, after years of hoping, trusting, waiting, and leaving the pen in God's faithful hands, the Author of romance scripted a new chapter in their love story. He made their future clear. They felt His gentle hand guiding them to serve Him together to reach the unsaved people of South America. They were married in a simple ceremony in Ecuador in 1953.

Was the sacrifice worth it? For all their waiting and radical decisions, did Elisabeth and Jim receive anything better in the end?

"I thank my God," Jim wrote shortly before their marriage. "I was recounting today how full He has made life for me. . . .

to know that we are wholly and for always committed to one another, sold out of ourselves each for the other's good. The absolute goodness and rightness of it is unspeakable. How shall I say what I feel in gratitude to God?"[2]

Elisabeth and Jim's love became a spectacular display of God's faithfulness and sovereignty. The decisions they made in their relationship prepared them for the adventure God called them to in their life together. They had learned sacrifice, self-giving, and implicit trust in their Creator. And soon these qualities would be put to an even greater test.

On January 8, 1956, Jim Elliot and six other missionaries were killed by Auca Indians—men whom Jim had diligently prayed for and sought to serve for six years. He willingly gave His life for the sake of Christ, and his example infused millions with passion for the gospel.

Elisabeth willingly surrendered her husband to Christ, just as she had done as a college girl in the auditorium that day. His faithful hand had scripted her story, and she knew that even in the midst of intense pain and heartache, His purpose was for her highest good.

After Jim's death, Elisabeth chose to give her life in service to the very people who had killed her husband, exemplifying the principle that she and Jim and built their marriage and life upon . . . "He is no fool who gives what he cannot keep to gain what he cannot lose."[3]

———————————

That is the kind of marriage we must help the younger generation discover. It's a love that withstands time and distance; a love that is willing to sacrifice *everything* for the greater love of Christ.

The kind of love that Elisabeth and Jim found cannot be sustained by human effort. It cannot be discovered through mere human emotion or physical attraction. It can be found only through two lives fully surrendered to the God of the universe. It can only be realized when two lives yield to the Author of romance Himself.

Christian marriages could be revolutionized if we would pursue this kind of love and teach it to our children. Trials, tragedy, and distance cannot quench the beauty of a God-written love story. The younger generation needs modern-day Elisabeths and Jims to follow. Are you willing to answer the call?

In a Nutshell

Building a successful relationship isn't the result of following a complicated formula or a set of moral guidelines. True relational success all comes down to one simple question: Who holds the pen of your life? And as true-love teammates for the younger generation, it's time we begin offering our kids the key to true success—*God Himself!*

When God holds the pen, He requests everything we are. He asks us to give Him complete control over every aspect of our lives. He beckons us to lay down our own agenda and let Christ overtake our being and live His Almighty life in and through us. He owns us, and He now operates our lives. It is no longer we who live, but Christ who lives in us. And such is the fuel for all life success, including romantic success.

As parents and leaders, your role is to introduce your children to the Author of romance so that they themselves can choose to give their pen to Him. You can't make the decision for them, but you *can* awaken them to the matchless beauty of a God-scripted life.

The Author of romance is eager and waiting to write an amazing love story for your child. Remember, He cares even more about this area of their life than you do as a parent. He doesn't just want to stand at a distance and offer His general blessing on your kids' lives and decisions. He wants to be intimately involved in every detail.

4

The Fire of a God-Written Love Story

*Helping kids discover heavenly love
that burns strong for a lifetime*

Leslie

Lifelong Faithfulness

A DIVORCE EPIDEMIC is attacking today's Christian marriages. Marriages are falling apart inside the church at the same rate as the rest of the culture. A recent study found that Christians actually have a *higher* rate of divorce than nonbelievers.[1]

Something is obviously missing from our training and preparation for marriage.

If we continue down this path, what will happen to the marriages of the future? Are we helpless against this escalating divorce trend? Should we just cross our fingers and hope it doesn't strike our children? Or is there something practical we can do to preserve the marriages of tomorrow?

As long as the next generation follows the same pattern that the older generation has followed, they won't experience a different result. It's like trying to make fresh orange juice out of

Kool-Aid powder. We can pray over our Kool-Aid, hoping that it will somehow turn into freshly squeezed orange juice. But as long as we keep using the wrong ingredients, we will keep ending up with the wrong result.

It's time to begin teaching the younger generation new patterns, giving them the *right* ingredients for marriages that will stand the test of time.

Current pattern: Faithfulness is viewed as something to be learned *after* the wedding vows. Young couples who have lived a self-focused existence are taking selfish attitudes into marriage. They haven't learned to love each other sacrificially *prior* to marriage, and they find it difficult to maintain lifelong faithfulness to each other *after* marriage.

God's pattern: Faithfulness is an art—a discipline that can be developed in young peoples' lives long *before* they ever meet their future spouses. We have an amazing opportunity to begin divorce-proofing our children's future long before they even meet their marriage partner. We can help them lay a foundation for a lifelong marriage by teaching them the art of lifelong faithfulness.

Lifelong faithfulness is so much more than an abstinence commitment. Lifelong faithfulness means being completely set apart—heart, mind, and body— for one person for a lifetime. It's learning to love someone with the very love of Christ—*sacrificially, selflessly, and unconditionally.*

> Lifelong faithfulness means being completely set apart—heart, mind, and body— for one person for a lifetime.

In God's pattern, faithfulness begins long before the wedding vows and continues to be cultivated for a lifetime.

Not long after I decided to give God the pen of my love life, I stumbled upon a life-changing principle from Proverbs 31:11, "The wife of godly character . . . brings her husband good and not harm all the days of her life." *All* the days of her life—those words seemed to pierce my heart. At sixteen, marriage seemed a long way off. I hadn't given much thought to honoring my future husband and doing him good *now*, even before I met him—*all* the days of my life. Sure, I'd saved my technical virginity for him. I'd followed the "Christian dating rules." But as I'd interacted with the opposite sex, I hadn't been seeking to honor my future spouse. I hadn't been setting my life apart for him.

Instead, I had followed the trend of the culture, casually jumping into one short-term fling after the next. I poured myself—heart, mind, and body—into every temporary relationship that came along. I gave my heart, my emotions, my mind, and even much of my physical purity to one guy after the next. And when each whirlwind romance ended, I was left devastated and heartbroken.

I'd heard a lot of teaching on saving my virginity for marriage. But I'd never understood that faithfulness to my future spouse was meant to be so much more. "What if my future husband could see me interacting with the opposite sex?" I asked myself. "Would he feel honored and loved by what I'm doing?"

The answer was clear.

When I read those words in Proverbs 31—*all the days of her life*—I realized that I had not being doing my husband good— I had been doing him harm. I had been giving pieces of myself to one fling after the next. I had been robbing from the treasure that belonged to him alone—the treasure of my heart, mind, and body. I had been squandering a precious gift that was meant for only him.

That day, I made a life-changing commitment. "The next time I enter a relationship with someone," I said to God, "won't be until I know he is the one that You have chosen for me to spend the rest of my life with."

I made the decision to begin doing my future husband good and not harm, *all* the days of my life. It became my goal to live faithfully for him, not just by keeping my physical virginity intact, but by guarding my heart, mind, and emotions as a sacred treasure for him alone.

To keep that commitment, radical changes had to be made. No longer could I build my life around the pursuit of the opposite sex. No longer could I casually jump into short-term flings. No longer could I spend my time and energy flirting and drawing guys' attention to myself.

I was now a one-man woman, set apart for one man—my future husband.

As I began to honor this man and live faithfully for him, he became more than just a distant person I would meet someday. He became the love of my life. Even though I didn't know his name and I couldn't picture his face, I began to love him. It wasn't an emotional love; it was a love based on commitment and devotion. It was the foundation for a lifelong marriage commitment based on trust and faithfulness. And it began before Eric ever came along.

Was it easy? Not at all. Watching my friends flit from one dating relationship to the next made me feel like I was missing out on a normal teenage experience. I often worried that the best years of my life would slip away. I feared that if I lived a fully set-apart life, I would never find someone to spend my life with. There were nights when I cried myself to sleep, asking God for the strength to live faithfully for my spouse in the midst of all my doubts and temptations.

Was it worth it to keep such a radical commitment? More than words can say! Giving up the temporary pleasure that came from short-term relationships was a small price to pay for what I received in the end.

Years before Eric knew me *he* began to live faithfully for *me*. He prayed for me—his future wife—every day. He lived as if I could see his thoughts and his actions toward other girls. He honored me in every aspect of his life. He even wrote me love songs and love letters as he waited for God to bring me into his life.

On our honeymoon, Eric gave me a precious gift—a notebook full of love letters that he had written to me years before we met. As I read page after page of his commitment to me, a commitment he made long before he met me, I knew that I didn't have to worry about his being faithful to me in our marriage. He had already spent years of his life being faithful to me before he even knew my name.

Are young people willing to make radical choices in order to honor their future spouses? Absolutely. Young people everywhere are catching the vision of lifelong faithfulness. They are making decisions to live set apart for their future spouses, even before meeting them. They aren't just focused on keeping themselves physically pure, but on honoring their spouse with their heart, mind, and emotions. They are choosing to love their future spouses even now, by honoring them with the way they live.

A young woman named Haley recently told us, "I write love letters to my future husband several times a month. It helps me see my future husband as a real person—not just a vague concept. It helps me remember to love him and honor him with the way I'm living right now."

A college sophomore named Jared said, "Even in my friendships with girls, I always pretend that my future wife can see my actions and thoughts. It's my goal to honor and love her at all times, even before I meet her."

It's this kind of faithfulness that can turn the tide of tomorrow's marriages. As we exchange the current patterns for God's patterns, we will begin to see a new generation of romances that stand the test of time.

THE DANGER OF SHORT-TERM FLINGS

When parents and leaders fail to pass on a vision for lifelong faithfulness, purity is often interpreted by Christian teens to be something like this: "While you are flitting around from one short-term relationship to the next, giving away your heart and soul to each one, at least save your technical virginity until marriage."

Too many parents and leaders see short-term flings as a normal part of the growing-up experience. Temporary romances are winked at and taken lightly, or even spurred on by unwitting adults. Parents often fail to realize that these whirlwind relationships shatter young hearts and ruthlessly sabotage the beauty of lifelong faithfulness to a future spouse.

Katie, a high school junior, recently told me about her frustration with this mentality among her youth group leaders. "Since I was fourteen, I've given my heart away at least six times in short-term flings with guys in our youth group," she said. "Every one of these relationships was encouraged by our youth leaders. They thought it was just harmless puppy love. But someone should have warned me what I was getting into. Every one of these relationships took something from me that I can never get back."

Today's short-term relationships mean something very different than yesterday's innocent soda fountain romances. Young people who are desperate to feel accepted are pouring themselves physically and emotionally into intense relationships that last only a few days, weeks, or months, but leave scars that last a lifetime.

Anna—a bubbly eighteen-year-old—met Justin at a Christian retreat. They began a serious relationship after knowing each other for less than a week. Their friends and family cheered on their whirlwind romance. On the outside, it seemed like a wonderful match—two attractive and outspoken Christian young people in a fun, fresh romantic relationship.

But looking closer, there were danger signs looming just below the surface.

Anna and Justin's relationship was physically and emotionally intense from the beginning. Anna soon became completely dependent upon Justin for her security, fulfillment, and happiness. When she was away from him even for a short time, she could hardly function in her day-to-day life. Whenever Anna and Justin were together, the physical side of their relationship quickly spiraled out of control.

Anna confided in her parents and close friends that she and Justin struggled with constant physical temptation. "God will give you the strength to stand for what you believe," some encouraged her. "Just make sure you have an accountability partner, and that will help you stay pure," others advised.

No one ever bothered to state the truth—that this relationship had taken an unhealthy hold over Anna's life. No one ever pointed out that emotion and physical passion were controlling their relationship rather than the Author of true love. To them, it seemed that Anna was following the normal path of a solid young woman. Both Anna and Justin were committed Christians. They were both committed to abstinence. What more could be expected?

After two months, Justin decided he was ready to move on. He ended the relationship with one abrupt telephone conversation. Anna was devastated. She fell into a deep depression and began floundering in her walk with God.

"I don't understand what went wrong," her mother lamented to me. "It seemed that she and Justin had such a healthy relationship. How could it have destroyed her life like this?"

But her criteria for a "healthy" relationship was sadly anemic. It only mattered that Anna and Justin were following the basic "Christian rules"—dating other Christians and committing to save sex until marriage. She didn't realize that rules were not enough to stand against the raging tides of physical passion and heated emotion (ee Colossians 2:20–23).

We must begin pointing the younger generation toward true set-apartness, rather than expecting them to settle for short-term flings. We must begin training our children to guard their heart as a precious gift for only one person, rather than carelessly throwing it to one relationship after the next. Let's teach them to honor and love their future spouse with the way they live, starting today.

MAKING IT PRACTICAL

> *True-Love Challenge #7*
> Your child is vulnerable to the culture's short-term relationship pattern.
>
> *The True-Love Answer*
> Help your child rise above the temporary-fling mindset.

A father of three young daughters recently told us, "We are raising three princesses in our home. We tell each of our girls that her heart is a precious treasure—that the only man worthy of that treasure is the man that God has chosen for her to spend her life with."

A mother of two teenage sons told us she continually challenges them to remain set apart for their future wives. "What if your future wife could see your actions toward girls?" she asks them. "What if she could see your thought life? Would she feel honored and cherished, or hurt and jealous?"

The younger generation longs for a beautiful, lifelong love story. When we show them that they can invest *even now* in the success of their future romance, they catch a vision for something truly worth waiting for. When the younger generation realizes that they can love their future spouse even now, faithfulness becomes a romantic adventure rather than a dull drudgery.

ACTION PLAN

Three Practical Ways to Tackle This Challenge in Your Life Today

1. **Brainstorm the right words to describe your child's future.** In the early formative years of your child's life, your words go a long way in helping shape his perception of his future. Take some time to write down your vision for your child's future love story so that you will be ready with the right words to say when the subject comes up. For example, instead of referring to the time when they will one day "start dating around," refer to the time when God will one day script a beautiful love story for them. Instead of talking about "all the boyfriends" or "all the girlfriends" they are going to have someday, talk about the "special person that God will bring into your life in His own perfect time and way." If you take some time to develop the right words to describe for what you want your child to discover, you won't be in danger of leading him or her down the typical cultural path by the words you speak in those early years.

2. **Show tough love when necessary.** If your teen is in an unhealthy romantic relationship, prayerfully consider how God might want you to step in as a protector. In some cases,

praying diligently might be the best course of action. In other situations, sitting down and confronting your child about his or her choices might be important. Be sure to be directed by God in the process and not merely your own emotion. Focus on expressing the nature and heart of Christ—not your own anger or hurt—in those tough conversations. Even if you must get uncomfortable, don't put your own ease above your child's future. Allow God to use you as an obstacle to keep your son or daughter from heading down a destructive path.

3. Study God's covenant relationships with your child. If your child is open to it, consider going through a Bible study on God's design for covenant relationships. God isn't into temporary flings. He doesn't date us for a weekend and then dump us on Monday. Rather, God builds lifelong covenant relationships with us. As your child gains a clear picture of His amazing design for covenant, he or she will gain an even greater understanding of what lifelong faithfulness is all about. (If you are looking for a practical way to start, we'd recommend the covenant study from Precept Ministries, www.precept.org.).

MAKING IT PRACTICAL

True-Love Challenge #8
Your child needs more than an outward understanding of faithfulness.

The True-Love Answer
Teach faithfulness that flows from within.

Does today's younger generation have an understanding of faithfulness from within? Let's take a peek into the life of a typical modern Christian young man—we'll call him Matt. Matt is active in his youth group and wants to go onto the mission field someday. He is passionate about Christ and eagerly shares the gospel with his unsaved friends. On the outside, Matt seems like the epitome of solid Christlike manhood. But inwardly, Matt harbors a secret. He struggles constantly with lustful thoughts and fantasies. An addiction to Internet pornography grips him like a vice.

"As a guy, you will always struggle with impure thoughts" is the subtle message Matt has always heard from other Christians. "You'll always have a fetish for the female body. It doesn't mean you are a pervert—it's just the way men are wired. Yes it's true, Matt, that you shouldn't become a Ted Bundy-like sex fiend, but you shouldn't beat yourself up over every lustful foible."

Since no one in Matt's life has raised the standard of inward purity, Matt has come to believe that his lustful addictions are normal. He hasn't learned how to honor girls in his thought life. The only thing he has learned is how to keep his sexual fantasies skillfully hidden behind a Christian act. If he were to be honest, Matt would admit that he has a hard time seeing young women as anything but sex objects. When girls walk by, his eyes automatically look them up and down. His mind automatically fantasizes about them sexually.

Matt has been in several dating relationships. Instead of honoring these girls and protecting their purity, he's pressured them to give in to his lustful desires. Though he hasn't "crossed the line" and given away his virginity, he's taken pieces of physical purity from one girl after the next.

Matt is extremely excited to get married someday, though not for the right reasons. He doesn't see marriage as God intended it to be—a beautiful expression of selfless love and faithfulness. Matt sees marriage as an opportunity to finally have his sexual desires fulfilled. He's not training in the art of lifelong faithfulness. He's training for lifelong selfishness.

Sadly, Matt isn't much different than most Christian young people his age. When selfishness is at the core of a young person's life and attitude, he cannot truly love his future spouse. No amount of Christian cover-up can replace *inner* purity and lifelong faithfulness.

When Eric was in college, God challenged him to begin honoring his future wife in every aspect of his life—not just to guard his physical purity for her, but to live as if she could see his thoughts and watch him interact with the opposite sex. He had to be completely retrained in the way he treated women— to see them as Christ's treasures rather than sex objects. He had to learn to jealously guard his mind—to kick out every thought that did not show honor and love to his future spouse.

His goal was to love his future wife even when she couldn't see him; even in the moments when no one else was watching, even in his most intimate meditations. It was not an easy skill to learn. But it laid an amazing foundation of trust and faithfulness in our marriage relationship today.

We must begin teaching young people about the kind of purity that flows from the inside out. Purity will be only a hollow, empty shell unless it stems from inner *selflessness* rather than inner selfishness. True faithfulness means a life *completely* set apart for one person—body, heart, and mind.

ACTION PLAN

Three Practical Ways to Tackle This Challenge
in Your Life Today

1. **Help young men gain God's perspective on inward set-apartness.** One of the biggest challenges for young Christian men in today's culture is keeping their thought life pure. From a shockingly early age, boys are bombarded with sexual temptations and pressure. Lust is a chronic problem for countless young men, and all too often they have never received any spiritual guidance to help them gain victory in this area. Fathers, as soon as you sense your son is ready, begin offering practical help and spiritual direction about godly sexuality through Bible study, discussion, prayer, and accountability. Mothers, if your son doesn't have a father who can fill that role, begin praying that God would show you a godly man who can help him, such as a pastor or godly mentor. (To facilitate the

process, we'd recommend going through Eric's book *God's Gift to Women* as well as Joshua Harris's book *Not Even a Hint*.)

2. Help young women gain God's perspective on inward set-apartness. In today's world, young women often have no idea how to guard their inner life, keeping their mind, heart, and emotions truly pure for their future spouse. It's all too easy for a young woman to buy into the pressure and temptations of the culture, giving her inner life over to romantic fantasies and obsessions. When she doesn't learn how to guard her inner life, it leads to flirting, dressing seductively, lustful fantasies, and settling for short-term flings. Countless girls are giving their hearts, minds, emotions, and bodies away to one guy after the next as they search for romantic fulfillment. As a parent, you can point your daughter toward something better. As soon as you sense that she is ready, begin offering practical help and spiritual direction in this area of her life. Help her catch a vision for the mystery and dignity of God-built femininity. (To facilitate this process, we'd recommend going through my book *Authentic Beauty* as well as Elisabeth Elliot's book *Let Me Be a Woman*.)

3. Establish a clear response to perversion. Often, the moral decline of a culture comes so gradually that we don't notice it until it's too late. Eric likes to call this the "shrinking bikini" principle. In the 1920s, bathing suits covered far more skin than they do today, and bikinis were unheard of. But as the decades went by, bathing suits began to slowly "shrink," covering less and less. Today they cover almost nothing. As the bathing suit got smaller and smaller, no one stood up to protest because the change happened so gradually. To avoid the "shrinking bikini" principle when it comes to our children's sexuality, we must create a healthy distress for sin in our homes. Rather than overlooking small displays of perversion, it's important that kids see your abhorrence to the warped mentalities of the culture. Your response to immorality helps define your children's sense of right and wrong and their understanding of righteousness and sin. Don't let allow your kids to grow up thinking that sexual slime is normal and acceptable. Rather, set an example for them by hating what God hates and loving what God loves.

MAKING IT PRACTICAL

> *True-Love Challenge #9*
> Your child needs practical ways to love his or her future spouse now.
>
> *The True-Love Answer*
> Train your child to be a heavenly romantic.

As young people mature and blossom in their sexuality, they experience a growing desire to express their sexuality. And, contrary to the Christian mind-set that most of us have grown up with, this isn't all bad. It isn't necessarily harmful for a child to long to share her life and her love with another human being. In fact, that simple longing, if properly directed, can be the foundation for a beautiful, lifelong love story. But it is harmful if she takes this hankering for love into her own hands and scripts herself a sex-at-thirteen lifestyle.

There is a healthy, godly way of directing these budding desires and there is a selfish, ungodly way. Train your children to take these "love hankerings" and use them as opportunities to invest in their future marriages rather than as temptations to destroy their current lives. Teach them the selfless way, not the selfish one.

The concept of romance is really the concept of thoughtfulness. It involves meditating on what would make someone else feel loved and cherished and then doing it. By helping your child harness these "love hankerings" into real-life opportunities to express thoughtfulness to his future spouse, you can not only help satisfy his newfound true-love longings, but also help him practically invest in his future marriage. You can teach him how to be a romantic even before he meets his future love.

There are so many things young people can do now, in their single years, to invest in their future married years. The simple question, What would make my future spouse feel loved and cherished? goes a long way to transforming a young person's perspective on this issue. A love letter? A love song? A love poem? The sky is the limit when it comes to what your kids *could* be doing for their future spouse even now, before they meet him or her.

ACTION PLAN

Two Practical Ways to Tackle This Challenge
in Your Life Today

1. **Encourage your child to become a romantic.** In today's world, it isn't easy for young people to live out lifelong faithfulness for their future spouse. Young people who have made this commitment need regular reminders of what they are waiting for. Encourage them with some practical and romantic ways they can invest into their future love life even now. Eric and I know quite a few young people who have begun keeping a notebook of love letters to their future spouse. Whenever they feel discouraged, impatient, or tempted to settle for short term flings, they take some time to write a letter of love and commitment to their future marriage partner. It helps them think of their future spouse as a real person, and helps remind them that they are learning to love that person even now. Encourage your child to explore creative ways of expressing his or her commitment, whether through writing love letters, composing love songs, keeping a hope chest (for girls), or simply praying a specific prayer each night for the person that he or she will one day marry. Faithfulness is a beautiful, romantic aspect of true love. Don't let your kids miss out on the amazing opportunity they have to invest today in their future marriage.

2. **Teach the "two eyeball principle."** A great way to encourage lifelong faithfulness is to teach your child how to live as if his future spouse could see his actions and thoughts. Eric and I like to call this the "Two Eyeball Principle." When

Eric was in college, he made a commitment to live as if his future wife's eyes were watching him interact with the opposite sex at all times. Even in his friendships with girls, he wanted his future wife to feel honored and cherished if she could see him. As your child seeks to live out his or her commitment to set-apartness, continually encourage her with this principle. If her future spouse would feel hurt or jealous because of the way she is dressing, thinking, or interacting with the opposite sex, that's a sign that something is off track. If her future spouse would feel loved and respected by the way she is dressing, thinking, or interacting with the opposite sex, that's a sign that she is living in true faithfulness for that person even now.

A Picture of Lifelong Faithfulness

Romania

1945

"Sign these divorce papers," said the man at Sabina's door. "Your husband is dead anyway. If you just sign these papers, you'll be able to obtain a ration card and buy food. Otherwise you and your son will starve to death."

Sabina rubbed her hand wearily across her eyes. It had been five years since her husband Richard was thrown into prison for being a pastor. She hadn't seen or heard from him in all that time. Was he really dead, as this government official said? Or was it just another Communist trick? She didn't know what to believe.

Sabina had recently been released from prison herself, where she had lived in abhorrent conditions, near starvation.

And now that she was free, she was a social outcast, unable to buy food, unable to take care of her son.

She knew if she cooperated with the government and signed divorce papers, she would be taken care of. No longer would she have to watch her son get thinner by the day. No longer would she have to throw herself on the charity of others just to survive.

But Sabina reminded herself that she had promised to stay faithfully by Richard's side in sickness and in health, for better and for worse. As long as there was even a chance he was still alive, she refused to break that sacred vow.

"Please leave," she told the man at her door. "I'm not going to sign those papers."

"You are making a terrible mistake," the man warned. "You won't be able to survive without a ration card. What a bad mother you are, to let your son starve to death!"

But Sabina was unmoving in her decision. "God will take care of us," she said firmly. "I will honor my commitment to my husband."

The months passed, and Sabina relied on God's provision. Somehow, she and her son managed to live and eat. But their life was incredibly hard, and Sabina was growing more and more weary trying to make ends meet. As the months rolled into years, Sabina began to lose hope that her husband was still alive. Time and time again, people came to her door to tell her that they had been in prison with Richard and that they had seen him die. There seemed little reason to keep waiting for him.

And then a new temptation came into her life. His name was Paul—a kind and gentle Christian man. As their friendship developed, Sabina knew Paul was falling in love with her. "Here is a man with whom I could build a new life," Sabina thought to herself many times. Paul wanted to marry Sabina, to care for her and her son. After almost ten years of being alone, the idea was very appealing.

"Let Richard go," her friends advised. "Your life has been hard enough. Marry Paul. You deserve some happiness after all you've been through.

Sabina did some serious soul searching and praying. Maybe she was being foolish to keep waiting Richard. Maybe he really was dead, as everyone told her. How much longer could she keep going this way?

But then Sabina felt God's gentle prick upon her heart. She loved Richard. It wasn't a love based merely on emotion, but on commitment and sacrifice. She had promised him lifelong faithfulness. Did she really have an excuse to break that holy vow just because her life was difficult?

As hard as the decision was, Sabina knew what she must do. Even as part of her heart broke, she told Paul that she could not see him anymore. She would wait faithfully for her husband for as long as God kept them apart.

And one day, just a few months later, she knew that she had made the right decision. As she scrubbed the floor of a church building, a friend came rushing in, waving a postcard. Richard's handwriting was unmistakable. He was alive!

Sabina knew prisoners were only allowed to write ten censored lines, if they were allowed to write at all. What would Richard say, after ten years of not knowing whether his wife and son lived, not knowing if Sabina was still waiting for him?

She read the words through tear-filled eyes. "Time and

distance quench a small love but make a great love grow stronger." Lovingly, she tucked the priceless message into her Bible, and read it over and over again during the months that followed.

And suddenly one day, Richard was home. As she opened the door of her flat, there he stood, looking more like a skeleton than a man. Hardly daring to breathe, she ran to him. As he put his arms around her, she nearly fainted. She couldn't believe she was finally in the arms of her beloved husband after ten long years.

The trials Sabina and Richard had faced only strengthened their love and devotion for each other. Shortly after Richard's return, they celebrated their twentieth wedding anniversary. They didn't have a penny to buy each other a gift, but Richard managed to obtain a pretty notebook in which he wrote verses every evening—love poems addressed to Sabina, the love of his life.

Richard and Sabina spent the rest of their lives laboring together on behalf of the underground church. They faced many more intense challenges and trials, including another six-year separation. But it served only to strengthen their love for each other.

At the end of her life, Sabina called her beloved Richard (who was also very ill) to her bedside. In the presence of a small group of friends, she told him again how much she loved him and asked him to forgive any shortcomings in her life. They held each other one last time. Then Sabina went to meet her Savior. A short time later, Richard joined her in eternity. [3]

That is the kind of marriage we must help the younger generation discover. It's a love that withstands time and distance, a love that is rooted in faithfulness, a love that is built around Jesus Christ. It's a love that only grows stronger and deeper throughout a lifetime.

The kind of love that Richard and Sabina shared cannot be sustained by human effort. It cannot be discovered through mere human emotion or physical attraction. It can only be realized through two lives fully surrendered to the God of the universe, when two lives yield to the Author of romance Himself.

Christian marriages would be revolutionized if we would pursue this kind of love and teach it to our children. Trials, tragedy, and distance cannot quench the beauty of a God-written love story. The younger generation needs modern-day Richards and Sabinas to follow. Are you willing to answer the call?

In a Nutshell

The modern understanding of marriage faithfulness is faulty. Faithfulness is considered something meant only for *after* the wedding vows and not *before*. And as a result, young couples who have never lived anything but self-focused lives are taking selfish attitudes into marriage. They haven't learned to love each other sacrificially *prior* to marriage and therefore find it excruciatingly difficult to love sacrificially once the vows have been exchanged.

But the art of marriage faithfulness wasn't meant to be a crash course learned in the first weeks of married life. Far from it! It was meant to be a lifelong training process begun long before young people ever meet their future spouse. And it's the responsibility of every parent and leader to articulate this amazing concept to their kids and to guide them toward the path of lifelong faithfulness.

Lifelong faithfulness is so much more beautiful and romantic than a mere abstinence commitment or a moral obligation. Lifelong faithfulness means being completely set apart—heart, mind, and body—for one person for a lifetime. It's the art of learning to love someone with the very love of Christ—*sacrificially, selflessly, and unconditionally.* And in God's economy, lifelong faithfulness is exactly that—*lifelong.* It's meant to begin long before the wedding vows and then continue throughout a marriage "till death do us part!"

When parents and leaders fail to offer a vision for

lifelong faithfulness, purity is often interpreted by Christian teens to be "just save sex until marriage." But there is so much more to give your child than moral guidelines. Let's give them a vision for a lifelong love story that can start this very day.

Part Three

PURITY THAT ENDURES

Train up a child in the way he should go: and when he is old, he will not depart from it.
—Proverbs 22:6 KJV

❖

Pure and undefiled religion in the sight of our God and Father is this: . . . to keep oneself unstained by the world.
—James 1:27 NASB

❖

"Do not handle! Do not taste! Do not touch!" . . . Such regulations indeed have an appearance of wisdom, . . . but they lack any value in restraining sensual indulgence.
—Colossians 2:21–23 NIV

❖

Put on the new man, which after God is created in righteousness and true holiness.
—Ephesians 4:24 KJV

5

THE KIND OF PURITY THAT ENDURES

Training kids to be in the world but not of it

Eric

THE BATTLE FOR PURITY

DANNY GREW UP IN A CHRISTIAN HOME. From an early age, his parents taught him all the right things about God, relationships, and purity. For many years, it seemed like Danny was on the right track. He remained a virgin throughout high school and lived a solid moral life throughout his teen years.

But during Danny's first year of college, something changed. His commitment to purity seemed to dwindle with each month that passed. He got involved with several girls who had very different standards than the ones he'd grown up with. And soon Danny's Christian values had flown out the window. He adopted a lifestyle of self-indulgence and immorality. When his parents confronted him, Danny merely shrugged and replied, "When I was growing up, you told me what to believe. But now I need to make my own decisions. And I've decided that I don't believe the same things you do anymore."

Sadly, Danny's story is not unusual. The younger generation is leaving Christianity in droves. Recent studies have shown that as many as three out of every four young people raised in the church have rejected Christianity by the end of their freshman year of college.[1] Researcher George Barna says that, in the last twenty years, today's churched teens have the lowest likelihood of holding on to their parents' spiritual values after leaving home.[2]

What is causing so many young people to snub their Christian heritage? How can young people who have grown up knowing truth so quickly reject it once they are on their own?

Our children are living in a polluted, twisted, and perverted world. That's the reality we must face. But the path our children choose once they leave home is not just a matter of chance. As parents and leaders, we must train our kids for *purity that endures*. We must give them the foundation that will sustain them long after they are living on their own and making their own decisions. We must build in them an understanding of true and lasting love. We must paint mental pictures for them of great love stories and the sublime grandeur of faithfulness.

Today's young people need to understand the battle over their soul. And more importantly, they must be equipped to fight that battle and actually win.

RIGHT DESIRE, WRONG METHOD

Years ago I attended a men's conference. The speaker posed an interesting question to the audience: "When you were growing up," he asked, "how many of you had fathers who talked to you about sex?" Out of a group of three hundred men, only five raised their hands.

Very few of today's parents were ever properly trained in the art of purity themselves, and as a result they have no established method by which to train up their own children for purity. When it comes to giving their children the right foundation for purity that endures, most parents feel like they are shooting in the dark.

When I was eleven, my parents were awakened to the growing pervasiveness of sexuality in our culture. After they watched a James Dobson film on adolescence, my parents hit the panic button. My dad realized that the time had come to have one of those man-to-man chats about sex with his soon-to-be-puberty-stricken-son. It was the last thing he wanted to do. How was he supposed to broach such an awkward subject with an eleven-year-old?

"Uh, Eric?" I remember him saying to me that fateful night. "Why don't we go for a drive?"

I was thrilled to spend the evening alone with my dad. I had no idea what I was in for.

My dad didn't know where to take me, so we drove around for a while in our family's banana-yellow VW bus. Not a word was spoken. My dad was in deep thought. I'm sure he was thinking, *Where in the world am I supposed to go for a conversation like this? A restaurant? No! A hospital? No! A cemetery? No!"*

We looped around our familiar streets a few times until finally he pulled into an empty parking lot in front of the local shopping center. He put our VW bus into Park and turned off the driving lights. Awkwardness filled the air. After all, we were in an empty parking lot, in relative blackness, at eight o'clock on a school night.

After an inordinate period of silence, my dad finally spoke. His voice was strained, and he shifted uncomfortably in his seat. "Uh, Eric, there's something I've been meaning to talk with you about . . ."

Still to this day that conversation holds the position as "most awkward father-son experience ever." I didn't say anything the entire time. My face turned beet red, and I just stared at the floor of the van as he talked. And when "the talk" was finally over, the subject of sex was never mentioned between us again. It was just too embarrassing and strange—not just for me, but even more for my poor dad!

> Purity, not merely innocence, should be our ultimate goal for today's kids.

Now that we are adults, my dad and I laugh about that night. I love my dad for giving it his best shot. His motives were right, but he was comically off-kilter in his method. My dad might have fulfilled his fatherly duty to help me understand the mechanics of my sexuality, but he didn't know how to help me understand the *purpose* and *possibilities* of my sexuality.

Right results hinge upon right method.

Loving, attentive parents are often wired for overreaction. They sometimes care so much for their kids that it can lead to comical extremes or just plain comical situations.

When I was seven, my mom heard the rumors about sugar intake being related to child rebellion. Immediately she grabbed a large, green trash bag, stuffed it full of everything in our refrigerator and pantry that even remotely tasted good, and hauled it out to our curb. For the next four months the Ludy kids endured flavorless plain yogurt, carob chips, and bowls of sugarless granola ad nauseum. And ironically, this miserable season of sugarlessness didn't quell my hankering for rebellion. In fact, it very well may have fanned it into flame.

My mom had the *right desire*—to purge potential rebellion from my life. But she utilized the *wrong method*—destroy the joy of eating food. When you, as a parent, come face to face with the awful reality of today's youth culture, there is probably an urge within you to pack your child into a freight container and ship him off to the northern regions of Iceland on the next barge. You have the *right desire* for your child—to keep him unstained in a polluted world. But to help him achieve God's very best, we must reach him with the *right method*.

PURITY VS. INNOCENCE

Many Christian parents I've talked with assume purity is similar to innocence; a total naiveté of perversion and sin. After all, if you don't know mustard exists, then it's awfully difficult to get it on your shirtsleeve. But contrary to popular belief, there is a big difference between purity and innocence.

Innocence is a naiveté of the world and its ways. It's an ignorance of immorality and the effects of sin upon a human life. Purity is something much different. Purity is the flexing of a moral muscle within a human soul, a moment-by-moment choice to walk a path of integrity amid a world polluted with sin. Innocence is a state of being. But purity is a *choice, a step of obedience, a decision of the will.* Purity, not merely innocence, should be our ultimate goal for today's kids.

A mother of three said to me the other day, "I want my children totally naive of the smut in this perverted world. My husband and I guard them, as best we can, from ever encountering the sinful pollution of this culture. But it's really hard!"

Helping kids stay innocent of the world's evil is certainly an important part of parental protection. *But innocence is merely the soil in which purity can grow.*

Every parent must protect a child's innocence as long as it is necessary, but parents must be ready to let the innocence melt away at the appropriate time, so that purity can take over and rule the soul.

The Stove

To a two-year-old, the kitchen stove represents only one thing—*a bad burn!* Any loving parent would say to their toddler, "Don't touch the stove!" We love our kids too much to let them get burned. We don't restrict them from the stove because we want to rob them of fun, but because we want to secure them a whole and healthy life.

A stove isn't bad in and of itself. But a stove in the hands of a two-year-old is a dangerous thing. As adults, we can use the stove daily, and it never poses a threat to our health. The difference between us and a two-year-old is obvious: we have the maturity to handle this powerful tool, while he does not.

Oh, how similar the issue of sexuality is! Awakening to the concepts of sexuality too early in life means only one thing to a young child—*a bad burn!* Sexuality isn't bad in and of itself, but it must be treated with the same caution with which you would handle a stove around your two-year-old. Before your child is ready to handle this powerful tool, he must have the necessary maturity.

This is what innocence is all about. Innocence is a buffer for a young child's soul. It provides a healthy blindness to a child, so that he is not awakened to the potent issues of life too early. Innocence is a practice field and training ground for inner maturity, and ultimately purity, to grow and develop.

Purity takes time to form in a child's soul. It needs to be exercised and trained like any other muscle. A season of innocence provides a young life the opportunity to cultivate and fully develop a strong purity. When innocence is cut short, a child's purity muscle is often too weak to handle the sudden barrage of sexual awareness. He becomes vulnerable to a very bad burn, just like a two-year-old trying to heat up some chili on the stove. A violated innocence thrusts a young child into a dangerous situation that God never intended for him to encounter at so young an age.

Building Butterflies

A caterpillar will always be a caterpillar unless it finds its way into a cocoon. A cocoon is the perfect picture of innocence. While a caterpillar is in the cocoon, it transforms. Its wings grow, and its body prepares itself for a whole new life. While a caterpillar is growing its wings in the cocoon, it isn't yet ready to use them.

Purity is much the same. As young children are trained for purity, taught to yield to God, obey God, and guard their hearts and minds, they are not fully prepared to flex this purity muscle until the season of innocence has finished its work. It is then, and only then, that those butterfly wings can open and flutter effectively in the open air of this world.

Many parents struggle with the idea of releasing their children into a life of purity. When we come face to face with the reality of the culture, it's easy to want to keep kids guarded in the cocoon for the rest of their lives. But what good is a cocoon unless it finally breaks away and releases the new creature to fly, no longer as a caterpillar (a child), but now as a butterfly (a young adult)?

Modern parents tend to err in one of two ways: either they never help build their child a cocoon of innocence, or they keep their child in the cocoon too long when their child needs to be spreading those purity wings and flying. Both extremes hinder true purity.

Let's discuss the two important phases of purity development:

1. The Cocoon of Innocence. This is the time in which a young life is kept naive of the world's ways, ignorant of immorality, and untouched by a corrupt culture. It doesn't mean that he doesn't know bad things exist and that there is an enemy of his soul, but he is protected from knowing too much, too soon.

But this cocoon phase isn't meant for protection alone. It is in this time of sheltering that young lives can begin training for purity. Kids can learn to develop a personal relationship with God—to yield to Him, listen to Him, and obey Him. They can learn how to think on noble and heavenly things and guard their hearts and minds from being overtaken by selfish tendencies.

2. The Release into Purity. This is the time in young lives when they are ready to understand the world, the actual battle for their soul, and the enemy's agenda to destroy their life. This is the time when warriors are built and formed—young men and women who understand the spiritual war and know how to fight it in the power of the Holy Spirit.

It is in this time that the government of young people's lives switches from *external* to *internal*. It is no longer their parents alone who control their moral choices; they now share this responsibility with their parents. And this is where the purity training throughout all those innocent years pays off.

THE COCOON OF INNOCENCE: CATCHING THE VISION

Without a season of guarded innocence, purity has no soil in which to grow strong and healthy. A cocoon of innocence provides a launch pad for success in a child's inner life and, therefore, in his or her outer life. Let's look at how some successful parents have tackled the challenges of the cocoon season in their child's life.

1. *Handling the Topic of Sex*

Meet Tom and Mary. They are the parents of three children between the ages of seven and ten. And they excel at the art of protecting innocence.

"We've learned not to panic when the topic of sex comes up in our home," Tom says. "We simply treat it as an opportunity to plant some great seeds. We tell our kids that sex is an exciting topic that someday, in the near future, we will get the chance to talk with them about."

"I told one of my daughters that telling her about sex too early would be like handing her keys to a Ferrari before she knew how to drive," Mary adds with a chuckle. "I think we're whetting their appetite in a healthy way. We don't ignore the issue, but we build up an expectation for something beautiful and exciting."

2. *Guarding Worldly Inputs*

Meet Jim and Terri. They are the parents of four children between the ages of nine and fifteen. They excel in the art of protecting innocence.

"Jim and I love movies," Terri explains, "but in our home, movies are a rare thing. When Aaron, our oldest, was two, we decided that we wanted to create a home atmosphere that would be conducive to spiritual growth. We want our kids to have their input from godly sources, and not from worldly sources. So we've had to greatly alter our behavior patterns. Instead of movies or television at night, we pull out games and good books. I'll be the first one to tell you it hasn't been easy. There have been many moments I just wanted to slap in a DVD and veg on the couch. But the benefit of guarding worldly influences is invaluable. Our kids are not like so many others that feed on the frenzy of the pop culture. Their eyes are on heavenly things, not earthly distractions. It's worth the sacrifice!"

Jim and Terri aren't just careful about movies. Television, the Internet, and music are just a few of the other areas that they keep a close guard over. They are vigilant to protect the hearts and minds of their children from being exposed to the warped ideas of the culture. Jim and Terri's kids are set apart for

God's purposes, not just because they have been trained for lives of godliness, but because they have a protected environment in which to grow and mature toward purity.

It's important to note that guarding worldly input is something that must continue even *after* the cocoon phase of a child's life begins to fade. As young people mature and are released into a life of purity, they still need a place of refuge to return to—a sanctuary that is protected from the slime and perversion of the culture, a haven that reinforces the reality of God's ways.

No matter what age your children are, it's vital to actively guard your home environment from the twisted agenda of the culture. Even certain "Christian" influences—books, music, magazines—can sometimes serve to undermine the standards parents have sought to uphold in their children's lives. Some Christian musicians have a haughty or sensual attitude, which serves only to "excuse" this same attitude in their young listeners. Some Christian magazines or books promote shallow Christianity or a temporary fling mentality, which serves only to justify unholy and unhealthy behaviors among their young readers. Make sure that *every* influence you allow into your home reflects the nature and character of Jesus Christ—not the debased attitude of our society.

3. *Addressing the Issue of School*

When it comes to fighting for the hearts and minds of today's kids, we can't ignore the impact of the school environment they grow up in. Many Christian parents are completely unaware of the perversion and filth that has crept into the halls of modern schools, attacking kids at shockingly early ages.

(Remember Leslie's stories from earlier in this book?) If the dangers at school are ignored, the time and energy you spend building a healthy home environment can be undermined the moment your child steps on the school bus.

Dean and Patti are the parents of five children between the ages of eleven and nineteen. They excel in the art of protecting innocence, particularly in the area of school.

"Patti and I decided long ago," Dean told us, "that the culture around us can't define how we raise our kids—*God* has to be the one in the driver's seat. We have done quite a few things over the years that fly in the face of conventionality, but we don't regret one of them. When Tommy, our oldest, was about to start third grade, we visited the elementary school, sat in on some classes, hung out in the hallways, and interviewed the principal. By the end of the day, we knew that it was not an appropriate environment for our boy to grow and mature in the ways of God."

"We went down the road to the local Christian school," Patti continued, "and went through the same motions and came out with the same conclusion. So we decided to teach Tommy at home during his third and fourth grade years. When our family moved two years later, we went through the same process, checking out the schools and evaluating the environment. In the small Texas town in which we lived, we felt that it was a healthy environment for Tommy to grow. So we felt comfortable having him attend public school there."

For each of their kids, Dean and Patti have made individual decisions based on their children's individual needs. They have put a high priority on guarding and protecting their children's innocence and spiritual development. They don't follow a pat formula when it comes to schooling decisions. But they believe in getting involved and truly understanding their children's daily environment. And more importantly, they believe in doing what is best for their children's spiritual lives and not just what's easiest for them as parents.

Releasing Kids into a Life of Purity

Innocence is for a season, not for a lifetime. There comes a time in every child's life when he is ready to take more of the weight of personal moral responsibility upon his own shoulders. He is ready to understand this world we live in, to be *in it* but not *of it*. He is ready to embark upon a life of purity.

As a parent, you can externally govern a child for only so long. A child must ultimately learn to govern himself, to make his own choices, and to determine his own course. Eventually, kids have to emerge from the cocoon. In fact, it would be unhealthy to keep them in it.

So how can parents know when the time is right for this transition? I like what my friend Mike says. "As an attentive parent you can't miss it. You see it in their eyes, hear it in their voice—they are asking to be released, eager to test their moral wings in this world. The cocoon just seems to open all by itself; I've never needed to pry it apart in any of my kids' lives."

You can be confident that if you desire what God desires for your children, He won't let you miss this all-important transitional phase. He will give you eyes to see it and ears to hear it coming.

It's important to clarify that releasing a child into a life of purity is not releasing him or her into a life of *independence*. At the age of twelve or thirteen, that is never a good idea. Rather, we must release them into a life of increasing *personal responsibility* and *self-governance*.

Your kids must learn the life of dependence on God, while still leaning on the strength and support of you as parents. Your voice must still ring with authority, and they still must abide by the moral format of your home. But instead of your doing all their moral decision work for them, now they must begin to choose obedience, respect, and honor as their code of conduct. Before, you were solely responsible for morally guarding them. Now they have the opportunity to share in that responsibility of submitting their lives to God, and guarding themselves.

THE RELEASE INTO PURITY:
CATCHING THE VISION

Let's look at how successful parents have facilitated their child's release from the cocoon of innocence into a life of purity.

1. *Initiating the Transition Phase*

Meet Joe and Karen. They are the parents of three children between the ages of twelve and sixteen. They excel at the art of releasing their children into a life of purity.

"When Kendall, our oldest," Karen says, "was thirteen, Joe and I began to sense that she was eager to spread her wings. She was ready to take on some of the moral weight and responsibility for her life. So Joe and I prayerfully did our best to help her begin to take steps in that direction. It started with small things, like allowing her to choose how to use her own free time and giving her a night each week where she could plan something with her friends by herself."

"As she continued to mature and make good choices, we let her have more and more rope," Joe adds. "Now, at sixteen, Kendall, is surprisingly free, she doesn't have a curfew, and she doesn't have a list of parent rules to abide by, like most Christian kids her age. But that's because she doesn't need them. She is actually far more intent on getting a good night's sleep than we would be for her, and she delights in living an organized life and shining her purity for the entire world to see. She takes her freedom seriously and has no intention of losing it."

2. *Talking About Sex*

If a child first hears about sex from the *right* source and *right* perspective, he or she will be far less likely to fall prey to the world's twisted spin on the topic. It's vital that we give our children the right message about sex before the culture gives them the wrong one. There is no magical age that is right for each child. But parents who are tuned in to their kids' emotional and spiritual development will be able to sense when the time is right.

You've already met Dean and Patti, parents of five children between the ages of eleven and nineteen. They excel not only in the art of protecting innocence, but also in releasing their children into a life of purity.

"Ah, the sex talk!" Dean chuckles. "Just calling it the 'sex talk' is part of the problem. It loses all its beauty with a name like that. When parents sit down to pass on information *about* sex rather than a vision for what their sexuality *can be* in their life, they miss the point of what every child really needs. I mean, sure it helps for kids to understand how their bodies work, but that's not the full story."

"We have fun with this issue in our children's lives," Patti adds, "It not an issue that God intended to be awkward and shameful. It's meant to be an earthly picture of a heavenly reality. God invented sex to be a celebration of love, not an embarrassing, secretive thing."

"When we sense the time is right, we take each of our kids out for 'The Night,'" Dean explains. "It's a time when Patti and I talk to them about their sexuality. For each of our kids 'The Night' has been a different experience. But for each of our kids it's been the same amazing experience. They all anticipate it and know it's coming. It doesn't happen at an exact age. Tommy was eleven. Amber was twelve. We design 'The Night' around each individual child. We took Tommy camping. We took Amber to a nice hotel and treated her like a princess. We took Lily to a castle in Scotland when we were there on vacation."

"We pass on to them a vision of a beautiful love story," Patty says. "We impart to them a picture of how incredible a future marriage can be, and the role they play in seeing that happen. It's not just an introduction to sexuality, but an awakening to the amazing opportunity they have in this area of their life."

After "The Night," Dean and Patti make themselves available for ongoing communication with their children in this area. They don't treat sex as a shameful or awkward subject. They are available to talk anytime their children have questions or struggles. They are serving as their children's teammates, and as a result they are setting their kids up for amazingly successful futures.

MAKING IT PRACTICAL

True-Love Challenge #10
The culture is out to destroy your child's innocence.

The True-Love Answer
Build a cocoon of protection around your young child's life.

Taking the time to build a cocoon of protection for your young child can seem like a big headache in your already hectic life. It's so much easier to look the other way and plead ignorance as your kids watch television unsupervised, play their friend's video games, or traipse unchecked around the Internet. It's just so much easier to look at what other parents are doing with their children and respond, "Well, they do it and they are Christian parents. Therefore, it's all right for me." But the issue isn't what is all right for you, but what is all right for your vulnerable and impressionable children. *And that is something that only you can know.* God desires your child to be prepared for a life of triumphant purity, but for that to happen, he or she must have a cocoon of innocence in which to build strong purity muscles.

It does take an extra effort to preserve a child's innocence. It does mean sometimes doing things that other parents may decry as extreme. And it often means getting uncomfortable in order to see that your child's inner life is well tended.

Give your child a season in which to build a healthy and

strong inner domain. A well-guarded season of innocence in a child's life is like a well-trained season of discipline in a soldier's life—both prepare him for the toughest of battles.

ACTION PLAN

Two Practical Ways to Tackle This Challenge
in Your Life Today

1. Think through answers to questions about sex. Don't be caught off guard when your young child asks you where babies come from or what the word *sex* means. Prepare an answer ahead of time so that you will be confident and ready with the correct response when the time comes. Like Tom and Mary, you may choose not to directly answer your child's questions about sex during this cocoon stage of their life. If that is the case, then be ready with an answer such as, "One day soon, when you are old enough, we will plan a special time talk about that." Taking your child's age and maturity into consideration, think through the kind of responses that will work best for him or her. Be prepared to the best of your ability, and then lean on God's guidance for specific direction when "sex questions" come up.

2. Address your child's school environment. Like Dean and Patti, make a focused effort to truly understand your child's school environment and evaluate whether or not it is a spiritually healthy place for him or her to be. Visit your child's school and get a feel for the atmosphere and attitude of the other kids and the staff. Study the curriculum being taught, especially in subjects such as health class/sex education. Be sure that the cocoon of innocence you are creating at home is not being stripped away by your child's school atmosphere. And if you sense that it is, be willing to do whatever it takes to protect your child's innocence in these critical developmental years. Like Dean and Patti, make your priority what is best for your child and not just what it easiest for you.

MAKING IT PRACTICAL

True-Love Challenge #11
You want to help your children embrace personal moral responsibility for their lives.

The True-Love Answer
Help your children strengthen their purity muscles.

You don't want to be making moral decisions for your children when they are twenty-eight years old! You want them to take hold of the same hunger for purity that you have for their lives. Wouldn't it be great if your kids turned out to be more serious about the direction, the nobility, and the character of their lives than you ever were? Ironically, that is the way it is supposed to be.

God desires kids, as they mature, to begin taking over the responsibility for their own souls. Parents function as a miniature replica of God in a young child's life. Children learn from their parents how to obey, trust, receive love, receive forgiveness, receive discipline, and a whole host of other important things. And all this to prepare them to understand the relationship they are meant to have with their heavenly Father.

As children enter the seasons of emerging adulthood, they are meant to transition from being under their parents' authority to God's, submitting to Him as their life's Master and Ruler. Parents function much like John the Baptist functioned in preparing the way for Jesus Christ. When it was Christ's time to take over, John said, "He must increase, but I must decrease" (John 3:30 NASB). This doesn't mean that you are of any less importance in your child's life, but merely that your role of moral authoritarian is drawing to a close, thus opening up a whole new season of deeper more intimate relationship with your child as a friend.

A child first must learn with external rules to obey and yield. But ultimately the external discipline of a parent is meant to be exchanged for the *inward* government of God Almighty over that young life. The pattern is: from rules to relationship. From being governed by earthly parents to being led by a heavenly Father. From resisting what is good and right to longing for what is pleasing to God.

The ultimate goal is that your children would be yielded wholly and completely to the God of the Universe, that His will would become their will, and that His life would become their life. A child reared for true love is one who has experienced the truest love while growing up.

ACTION PLAN

Three Practical Ways to Tackle This Challenge in Your Life Today

1. **Give your kids God's perspective on sex.** Many parents think that the longer they can hold off talking with their children about sex, the better off their children will be. But if you don't get to your kids with God's perspective on sex at an early age, the culture will get to them first. Prayerfully evaluate your child's life and maturity level and decide the best time to talk with him or her about sexuality, keeping in mind the early influences of the culture. Like Dean and Patti, be creative in your approach. Talking about sex shouldn't be a clinical, awkward conversation, like the one with my dad in our banana-yellow VW bus. Rather, it should be a joyful, beautiful, exciting topic. When God speaks about sexuality, He uses the highest form of language—poetry. (See Song of Solomon.) If kids start out with the right perspective on sex, they will be far less likely to succumb to the wrong perspective further down the road.

2. **Gradually give your child freedom.** Prayerfully think about a specific area in which your son or daughter can practice taking personal responsibility in his life. Under your watchful eye, allow him to take charge of that aspect of his life. As your kids make godly choices and good decisions, be sure to offer them the praise and encouragement their behavior warrants, and reward them with even greater freedom. As you see them continue to mature and make consistently good decisions, give them more and more rope. Leslie's parents practiced

this approach with her two brothers. By the time the boys were in high school, they were making most of their own decisions and living responsible, godly lives. They were some of the only young people in their youth group that didn't have a curfew—because they didn't need one. They had learned how to govern their own lives with maturity and integrity, and therefore their parents didn't need to constantly police them. Begin offering your child gradual freedom, rewarding his good choices, and allowing him to fully embrace personal responsibility as he grows up.

3. Be available for ongoing communication. Even though you are encouraging your child toward a life of personal moral responsibility, he or she will still need your guidance and support along the way. Your child isn't yet ready to be fully independent. So be sure to stay alert to the spiritual, emotional, and physical needs in his or her life. Make yourself available to offer counsel, caution, or correction as God leads you. Facilitate regular discussions about their cares and concerns, and make sure your kids still have a parental pillar of strength to lean on.

In a Nutshell

There is a vast difference between innocence and purity. And it's critical that every parent understands the difference.

Innocence is naiveté of the world and its ways. It's ignorance about immorality and the effects of sin upon a human life. *Purity is something much different.* Purity is the flexing of a moral muscle within a human soul, a moment-by-moment choice to walk a path of integrity amid a world polluted with sin. Innocence is a state of being. But purity is a *choice, a step of obedience, a decision of the will.* Purity, not merely innocence, should be the ultimate goal for your children.

Every parent must protect a child's innocence as long as it is necessary, but every parent must be ready to let the innocence melt away at the appropriate time, so that purity can take over and rule the soul.

Purity takes time to form in a child's soul. It needs to be exercised and trained like any other muscle. A season of innocence provides a young life the opportunity to cultivate and fully develop a strong purity.

Modern parents tend to err in one of two ways: either they never help build their child a cocoon of innocence, or they keep their child in the cocoon too long when their child needs to be spreading his or her purity wings and flying in this world. Both extremes hinder true purity.

Yet if, as a parent, you can provide your child with

both the cocoon of innocence as well as a timely release into a life of personal moral responsibility, then you will have laid a foundation for a purity that will endure—a life able to be *in the world* but not *of it*.

6

THE CATALYST FOR PURITY THAT ENDURES

*Giving kids the right motivation for
living set-apart lives*

Eric

THE CHORE MENTALITY

LIKE MANY KIDS, I hated chores when I was young. I remember groaning as my mom announced my daily duties. Even going to the doctor for a shot sounded better than dusting bookshelves and making my bed. But though I despised my chores, I still did them. Why? Because if I didn't . . . *punishment awaited!*

When it was my turn to clean the kitchen I would slink over to the sink with a moan that sounded akin to a cat in heat. I would blurt out comments like, "How come I always get this job? The kitchen looks fine the way it is! I'm supposed to be meeting Brian down at the park to play basketball!"

A chore always represented one very clear thing to my mind: *opposition to something I really wanted to be doing.*

But, no matter how upset I might be, the fear of punishment gave me enough motivation to do the job. I must admit, however, that I didn't do my job very well. In fact, I did the absolute bare minimum. I would splash some water around in the sink, knock off a few hefty pieces of food from the plates, and then announce, "I'm done!"

My mom would come in and survey my paltry efforts with a sigh and say, "Eric, cleaning the kitchen involves more than putting the dishes in the dishwasher, it also means cleaning the counter!"

I would again let out another dramatic groan and wait for my mom to leave the kitchen. When she was out of sight, I would dampen a washcloth and polish a few random spots on the counter where it was obvious that there was a stain. Then I would again yell, "I'm done!"

"Eric, what about polishing the sink?"

I would give it a half-hearted swipe and declare, "I'm done!"

"How about putting away the tablecloth and placemats?"

I would shove them halfway into their drawer and shout, "I'm done!"

Time and again we would repeat this ridiculous process. In my efforts to make the chore painless and quick, I made it more and more miserable and interminable.

Finally, after an hour had passed, and my mom was totally exhausted by the ordeal, she'd relent, "Okay, you can be done!"

I'd breathe a sigh of relief and run out of the kitchen, thrilled to have my life back.

Unfortunately, the above-mentioned scene is a perfect portrayal of how most Christian young people today view restraining their sexual impulses. They view purity as a chore rather than an opportunity. The reason that many concede and actually do the job is not because they *want* to, but because they feel they *have* to. A threat of punishment looms above their heads, and they dare not anger or disappoint God, their parents, or their spiritual leaders.

All these Christian rules and limitations are deemed an obstruction, an opposition to something they really want to be experiencing. They want to be exploring their sexuality and experiencing what everyone around them is talking about. Instead, they groan their way through their young adult years, doing the absolute bare minimum required.

A rule-based foundation will gradually crumble as a young person gets older. Rules aren't enough to keep young people on the right path as they venture out on their own in this world.

Releasing a child into a life of purity can work only when that child has the right motivation behind their choices and commitments. All too often, parents focus on teaching the mechanics of purity but fail to help cultivate the things that make purity last.

Having the right internal motivation is what leads to the right external decisions.

RECIPES FOR WOE

The threat of punishment is just one of the methods parents have used for years in an attempt to rescue their kids from the sexual pollution of the culture. Below is a short list of the age-old favorites:

- **Scare Tactics**—"Hey Joey! Look at this picture of a man suffering from syphilis! If you're not careful, you could be next!"

- **Ignorance**—"I never talk about sex with my kids, because I figure that if they never learn about it, they will never be troubled by it."
- **Outright Lying**—"Sex is miserable! Boy, I wish I had never had sex! The only good thing that ever came out of it was you kids!"
- **Rules**—"I don't ever want to see you even look at a girl, son! I don't want you going to movies, listening to music, hanging out with friends, or shopping in grocery stores where they have all those girly magazines in the check-out aisle. You must never even get close to that stuff! 'Cause if you do, there'll be hell to pay!"

Interestingly, these above-mentioned methods actually work, at least to a certain degree. The power of fear and the numbing agent of naiveté are often effective in slowing the spread of immorality. But these ways, even with their apparent success, clip the wings of romantic love's beauty. They may work in helping a young person abstain from having sex, but they don't succeed in imparting a vision for a marriage that is a taste of heaven on earth. They don't train up a life for true inner purity.

Just as the threat of punishment motivated me to clean the kitchen, and just as Ulysses found that tying himself to the mast helped him pass the Sirens' coastline, so these methods can function mechanically in a human life to preserve an outward purity. But they do nothing to give our kids a foundation for purity that will last long after they are out on their own. And they do nothing to help our kids learn the sweeter song of God's ways.

Cleaning the Kitchen a Different Way

This may seem hard to believe after my previous description of my kitchen-cleaning adventures, but when I was young there were a few times when an angelic Eric Ludy emerged. Well, okay, maybe it only happened one time. My mom was out doing errands, the kitchen was dirty, and I got a strange idea.

I want to do something special for my mom!

I went into the kitchen with an odd excitement to clean it, scrub it, and polish it.

As I cleaned, I pictured my mom entering the kitchen when she returned home and being overwhelmed with joy that I'd cleaned it without being asked. And strangely, I found that the very job I hated as a chore was an amazing delight when I did it as an expression of love for my mom. As a chore, the job felt like cruel and unusual punishment. But as a gift of love, it morphed into a fun and exciting opportunity to bless my mom.

It's amazing how life's most difficult tasks can be completely transformed when they are done with the right motivation. Not only did this extraordinary method enable me to actually enjoy the process of cleaning the dreaded kitchen, but I also found myself going the extra mile to polish every last square inch of it. When I was done, the chrome fixtures were shining and the counter was spotless. And when my brother came in to get himself a glass of water, I shooed him away to protect my perfectly clean environment.

There are many ways to motivate young people to restrain from sensual indulgence. But there is only *one way*, prescribed by God, to train a young life for purity that endures.

Contrary to popular belief, God's method isn't to scare us or threaten us into obeying. He isn't afraid of sexuality as if it were a disease, and His intent isn't to bind us in legal misery with a whole list of "thou shalt nots." He has a much better way of motivating his children toward excellence. He gives us hope, vision, and a promise of a blessed future. He motivates us with the tool of a love relationship. Not a rule, not a threat, not a lie . . . *a relationship.*

RULES VS. RELATIONSHIP

I'm a happily married man, and I don't flirt with girls. You might be thinking, *I should hope not!* And you are right. It's good that I don't flirt with girls as a married man. But it's important to note *why* I don't flirt with girls. There are many different motivations that I could have. There's the "God says I shouldn't defraud a woman" reason, the "thou shalt not commit adultery" reason, and we can't forget the "selfishness is a sin" reason. Those are all fine reasons for not flirting with girls as a married man. But they hardly hold a candle to the actual reason that I've made this decision.

I'm motivated by something far more powerful, far more substantial than duty or obligation. *I'm motivated by my love relationship with Leslie.*

I love my wife so much. I desire to do good things for her. I look for ways to serve her, to make her smile, to make her feel confident and beautiful. I want her to know that she is my girl, that she holds my heart, and no other girl ever has even a chance of stealing my affections from her.

Since that is the way I feel about Leslie, why in the world would I flirt with other girls? My intense love for Leslie automatically cancels out the issue of flirting. I choose to live faithfully for Leslie not because it's required of me as a husband, but rather because I am wildly in love with my wife. It's as simple as that.

If you were to ask me why I choose not to look at pornography, I could give you many biblical reasons. It would be easy to govern my life around rules. But that is a miserable way to live. I don't indulge myself in pornography because of my intense love for both my wife and my God. I don't want to allow anything to ever interfere in those all-important relationships in my life.

Why do I study the Bible? Why do I pray? Is it because I am required to as a Christian? Am I afraid of awakening God's anger? No! It's because I love my God so much, I want to draw closer and closer to Him, becoming more and more acquainted with Him each and every day. It's *love relationships* that motivate me to do the right things—not rules, not threats, not lies, and not fears. I want to learn of my God and share my every waking moment with Him.

Being motivated by relationship, not rules, is the secret to finding the smile in our Christian walk. This is where the joy is found in what otherwise is a miserable chore. This is what Christ came to give us—*a new motivation for living.* Not law, *but love.* Not rules, *but relationship.* Not fear of punishment, *but opportunity to grow.*

In 1st Corinthians 13:1–3, the famous chapter on love, Paul expresses the importance of this concept:

> If I speak in the tongues of men and of angels, but have not love (as my motivation), I am only a resounding gong or a

clanging cymbal. If I have the gift of prophecy and can fathom all mysteries and all knowledge, and if I have a faith that can move mountains, but have not love (as my motivation), I am nothing. If I give all I possess to the poor and surrender my body to the flames, but have not love (as my motivation), I gain nothing. (Parenthetical statements added.)

The right decision, when disconnected from the right motivation, produces a wrong result. It's not enough to train our kids to do the right things; we must give them the *right motivation* to do the right things. We must help them discover their own love relationship with Christ and their future spouse. And when they make that discovery, they will hold the secret to purity that stands the test of time. Teach children to love their future spouse, and they will go far beyond mere abstinence commitments. Teach children to love their God, and they will go far beyond memorizing scriptures for Bible quiz team on Sunday nights.

MAKING IT PRACTICAL

True-Love Challenge #12

You want to help your child gain the right motivation for purity.

The True-Love Answer

Point your child back to Christ.

When young people come to Leslie and me seeking advice, it would be easy for us to give them a quick strategy or solution to their problem. But what they really need is a push toward the One who cares more about their lives than we ever could. They need to fall on their knees before Him and seek His guidance, His direction, and His purpose for their situation. They don't need human answers; they need heavenly perspective.

Parents and leaders have an amazing opportunity to point their kids to Christ on a daily basis. This doesn't mean we should never give them specific advice, but rather that we should first and foremost encourage them to pursue His heart and direction above all else. Children and teens are far more capable of developing an authentic, real-life relationship with God than most of us give them credit for. Encourage your kids to build their lives around Christ, to spend time daily seeking Him and listening to His voice, and to become intimately acquainted with the Lover of their soul.

ACTION PLAN

Three Practical Ways to Tackle This Challenge in Your Life Today

1. Remind your child often about God's heart for her. Leave little notes on your daughter's pillow periodically, reminding her about God's purpose and plan for her life. Write out a prayer of blessing for your son and have it framed as a gift of encouragement. Let your child hear the specific prayers and dreams God has laid on your heart for him or her. The more your children are reminded about God's heart for them, the more likely they will be to live a life fully abandoned to the One who loves them more than they can comprehend.

2. Develop the habit of turning to God first. Whenever your child has a problem or challenge, habitually encourage him to turn to God before any other action is taken. When you take the time to pray with your child and help him surrender every situation to God, you train him to lean on God above anyone or anything else.

3. Spend time praying and worshiping God as a family. When your children see you adoring your King, they gain a clear picture of the kind of relationship they themselves can have with God. Don't just talk about Christ in your home. Plan regular times to pursue Christ together as a family, whether through corporate prayer, family worship, or regular times of studying His Word together.

MAKING IT PRACTICAL

True Love Challenge #13
You want your child's purity to stand the test of time.

The True-Love Answer
Pass on the vision for a love-based purity commitment.

The ever-popular question being asked in youth groups across this country is "How far is too far?" Young people want to know how much physical contact with the opposite sex is okay with God. As parents and leaders, we often try to give them guidelines to help answer that question. We fail to realize that if young people are even asking that question, they lack the foundation for purity that endures.

A young person's focus shouldn't be on how much he or she can get away with. That's selfish motivation; purity based upon a rule and not a relationship. And rather than catering to this self-focused mentality, we must begin offering young people the right motivation—love for Christ and for their future spouse. Let's begin teaching them to ask a new question: "How far can I possibly go to please God in this area of my life?" Let's begin teaching them to love their future spouse even now by honoring that person in their daily decisions. Unless they are motivated out of love for Christ and love for their future marriage partner, their purity will be nothing but an empty shell.

ACTION PLAN

Two Practical Ways to Tackle This Challenge in Your Life Today

1. Facilitate a commitment ceremony. When the time is right and your child is ready, plan a special evening to make his or her purity commitment official. Be creative in your approach. Whether you take your child out for a nice dinner, hold a prayer ceremony in your living room, or invite a few close friends over as witnesses, the important thing is to give her an opportunity to express her individual commitment to set her life apart for God and her future spouse. It's also a great idea to give your child something memorable and special to symbolize her commitment. There are many creative ways to do this. Many parents give promise rings or a framed copy of their child's commitment, but we encourage you to customize your gift to your child in the way that best fits him or her.

2. Help your child plan a true-love project. Encourage your child to begin working on an outward expression of his inward love commitment to God and to his future spouse. Let him use skills he may have in carpentry, creative writing, music, art, etc. to craft something symbolic that will remind him of his commitment to the set-apart life. I know a young man who wrote and recorded a song for his future wife. I met a young woman who painted a beautiful picture expressing her desire to live a set-apart life. Encourage your children to savor the beauty of waiting and trusting by pouring their creative gifts into outward expressions of their inner love for Christ and for their future spouses.

In a Nutshell

There are many ways to motivate young people to restrain from sensual indulgence. But there is only one way, prescribed by God, to train a young life for purity that endures.

Contrary to popular belief, God's method isn't to scare us or threaten us into obeying. He isn't afraid of sexuality as if it were a disease, and His intent isn't to bind us in legal misery with a whole list of "thou shalt nots." He has a much better way of motivating His children toward excellence. He gives us hope, vision, and a promise of a blessed future. He motivates us with the tool of a love relationship. Not a rule, not a threat, not a lie . . . *a relationship*.

Being motivated by relationship, not rules, is the secret to finding the smile in our Christian walk. This is where the joy is found in what otherwise is a miserable chore. This is what Christ came to give us—*a new motivation for living*. Not law, *but love*. Not rules, *but relationship*. Not fear of punishment, *but opportunity to grow*.

The right decision, when disconnected from the right motivation, produces a wrong result. It's not enough to train our kids to do the right things; we must give them the *right motivation* to do the right things. We must help them discover their own love relationship with Christ and their future spouse. And when they make that discovery, they will hold the secret to purity that stands the test of time, as well as the secret to living a life full of the richest joy.

Part Four

TRUE-LOVE TRAINING

Fix these words of mine in your hearts and minds; . . . Teach them to your children, talking about them when you sit at home and when you walk along the road, when you lie down and when you get up. Write them on the doorframes of your houses . . . so that your days and the days of your children may be many in the land that the LORD swore to give your forefathers.
—DEUTERONOMY 11:18–21

❖

Fathers, do not exasperate your children; instead, bring them up in the training and instruction of the Lord.
—EPHESIANS 6:4

❖

7

THE LASTING POWER OF TRUE-LOVE TRAINING

Investing today in the marriages of tomorrow

Leslie

TRAINING YOUNG MEN AND WOMEN FOR PURITY that endures is only the first step in preparing them for successful relationships. If we want this generation to experience world-class marriages, we must also train them in the art of world-class love.

When Eric was growing up, his mom used to tell him, "Son, the way you treat me is the way you are going to treat your wife someday."

"I'm gonna treat her better than that!" Eric countered confidently. Like many in the younger generation today, Eric didn't see the correlation between the way he was treating his current family and the way he would treat his future family. He knew he was often insensitive and disrespectful toward his mom. But he reasoned that once he got married, those flaws would somehow melt away, and tenderness and respect for his wife would come naturally.

Anyone who is married knows that logic doesn't stand! Marriage doesn't naturally bring out our selfless, servant-hearted side. In fact, it often brings out our very worst! Today's Christian marriages are often full of selfishness and pride rather than serving and giving.

But mediocre marriages don't need to be the norm. We can help our children experience something so much better in their future, by *training them for true love* in the here and now.

If your daughter had a dream of winning an Olympic medal, you wouldn't expect her to start practicing her sport only a few weeks before the Olympic Games. Instead, you would help her devote years of her life to her event. You would wake up before dawn to take her to practice, you would hire the best coaches and teachers, and you would continually cheer her on as she honed her skill.

All of us want our children to win the Olympic gold when it comes to their future marriages. Yet, how many of us help them train to be the best they can be in this area of their lives? How often do we provide them with the coaching, the discipline, and the encouragement they need to go the distance?

Do our kids have what it takes to remain faithful to their spouse through intense trials and separation, like Richard and Sabina Wurmbrandt? Will their love be a world-changing display of forgiveness and sacrifice, like Jim and Elisabeth Elliot?

Instead of merely offering kids a few weeks of marriage counseling before they walk down the aisle, let's begin offering them *lifelong marriage training*. Let's help them learn the attitudes, motivations, and disciplines that will help them win the gold.

What would happen if young men were trained as Christlike warrior poets, men who heroically protect femininity instead of selfishly conquering it? What would happen if our young women were trained as Christlike princesses, women who jealously guard their feminine mystique and inspire men towards greatness?

What would happen if young people learned the art of selfless, Christlike love?

We would begin to see a generation of marriages that are a little taste of heaven on earth, marriages that only grow stronger and more beautiful through the challenges of life, marriages that leave a legacy for generations to come.

We have an amazing opportunity to groom the up-and-coming generation in the art of true love, long before they ever meet their future spouse. There is an incredible practice ground *right in our own homes.*

If young people can learn to be selfless and Christlike in their *current* family, they will have the right foundation to be selfless and Christlike in their future family. If young people can gain a clear picture of lifelong love in their *current* home, they will have a clear picture of God's design for lifelong love in their *future* home.

Let's look at some practical ways in which you can begin preparing your child for true love, starting today.

The Art of Tenderness

Christ gave us the ultimate model for true love. He left His royal throne and became one of us, looking at life through our eyes. He put aside His own rights in order to meet our deepest need. He selflessly sacrificed His life for his bride.

He excelled in the art of tenderness.

It's easy to meet another person's need the way we think it needs to be met. But tenderness means getting outside of our own perspective and looking at life through the other person's eyes, just as Christ did for us.

When I tell Eric that I need to get out of the house, he can respond in one of two ways. He can glance up from his work and absentmindedly suggest that I go take a walk. Or he can study my life, look at my *true* need for refreshment and companionship, lay aside his own agenda, and take me out for a special evening. Only someone skilled in the art of tenderness can understand the vast difference between these two responses!

> Tenderness means becoming a *student* and a *servant* of another person's life, looking at life through their eyes and meeting their needs exactly as they need them met.

Tenderness means becoming *a student* and a *servant* of another person's life, looking at life through their eyes and meeting their needs exactly as they need them met. Tenderness means setting aside our own agenda, laying down our own rights, and sacrificially serving someone else.

Tenderness is the secret to a marriage that sparkles and shines for a lifetime. When two people learn to love each other like Christ loved us, laying down their own selfish agenda in order to serve each other, they have found the ultimate recipe for true love that stands the test of time.

Tenderness isn't something to teach young people only

when they are about to walk down the aisle. It's something that we can cultivate and develop within them throughout their entire life. Yet most of us miss the opportunities that are right in front of us.

Jason is a young man who is truly passionate about Christ. He's active in his youth group and leads an after-school Christian club for athletes. When Jason is in public, he is sensitive to others, well-mannered, and even servant-hearted.

But as soon as Jason goes home, it's a different story. During a typical evening with his family, Jason yells at his brother, argues with his mom, ignores his dad, and taunts his sister. Within the walls of his home, Jason lives with a self-focused attitude. He is constantly fighting for his own comforts, his own agenda. He doesn't spend much time considering the needs and desires of the other four members of his family.

It's not that Jason is intentionally treating his family members with disregard. Jason is typical of most Christian young people today; he's grown up believing that it is normal for siblings to constantly fight and tear each other down. He's grown up assuming that continual family tension is just a part of life. He's never been taught that family relationships are his practice ground for future success.

What happens when Jason takes these attitudes and habits into his future marriage? Instead of being prepared to love and serve another person, Jason is far more prepared to love and serve himself. He is aiming for marriage mediocrity rather than marriage victory.

Jason represents an entire generation of Christian young people who are lacking in the art of tenderness. As parents and leaders, let's help our kids aim higher.

Instead of expecting kids to fight and tear each other down, let's begin teaching them to love each other like Christ loves. Instead of allowing tension and conflict to be the norm in our homes, let's start cultivating an atmosphere of selflessness and forgiveness. If we help them excel in the art of tenderness now, they will be on their way to a lifetime of true fulfillment.

RAISING WARRIOR-POETS AND PRINCESSES OF PURITY

When I was ten, the boys at school started acting differently toward the girls. Whether through the eye-opening effects of sex education class, the influence of the media, or the example of their dads and older brothers, the boys were learning how to treat girls as sex objects.

"Katie's de-vel-op-ing!" one of them would blurt obnoxiously, pointing at my friend Katie's chest with raucous laughter. "She has to wear a training bra!"

"But look at *that* ugly chick," another would howl as the boys scrutinized me, "she's flatter than the plains of Kansas!" More hysterical laughter followed his outburst.

Instead of being carefree fifth-graders focused on playing hopscotch and red rover, we became immersed in a "battle of the sexes." The boys were under constant pressure to prove their manhood by treating girls like objects. The girls were under constant pressure to prove their worth by being found attractive in the eyes of the opposite sex.

Many of the girls—some as young as ten or eleven—began dieting, dressing in miniskirts and halter tops and even developing eating disorders. Many of the boys—some as early as sixth grade—began carrying condoms in their wallets, proudly showing their friends that they were ready to "conquer" a girl when the opportunity came.

By the time I reached high school, the thought of finding a gallant young gentleman who would heroically protect a woman's virtue seemed laughable. And the idea of finding a virtuous young woman who called men to a higher standard was just as unlikely. Each sex had been trained to tear down the other.

Young men didn't know how to honor or respect femininity, only how to treat girls like pieces of meat to be devoured and spit out. Young women didn't know how to honor or build up masculinity; they used their sexuality to manipulate and control guys in order to get what they wanted.

This pattern is all too prevalent in today's sex-at-thirteen generation. Guys are becoming perverted "burpers and scratchers" out to conquer girls. Girls are becoming sexual manipulators out to conquer guys.

Even Christian young people are falling prey to this cultural trap.

Andy, a Christian teen who has grown up in church, recently told Eric, "I have no idea how to treat girls as sisters in Christ. I don't know how to encourage them to become virtuous women. When I see a girl, I automatically think of her in a sexual way."

Jessica, a Christian high school sophomore, told me that the idea of encouraging young men toward purity is a foreign concept to her. "All the guys I've met are obsessed with sex," she said. "I feel like the only way I can get a guy's attention is to flaunt my sexuality. I know I'm just feeding the problem, but I don't know how to interact with guys in any other way."

If we are to invest in the marriages of tomorrow, we must begin training the next generation how to build up the opposite sex rather than tear it down. We must teach our children to approach the opposite sex *selflessly* rather than *selfishly*. We must raise up a generation of warrior-poets and princesses of purity—young men and women who honor each other and treat each other like Christ would.

The training ground begins at home.

When a young boy learns to honor his mother and sisters, he learns how to treat women as Christ would treat them. When a young girl learns to honor her father and brothers, she learns how to treat men as Christ would treat them.

MAKING IT PRACTICAL

True-Love Challenge #14
You want your child to develop tenderness in the early years.

The True-Love Answer
Turn daily life opportunities into true love lessons.

Today's kids are growing up in a world with a warped mentality of how to treat the opposite sex. From television to movies to magazine covers—and even the influence of other kids on the playground—kids are being trained how to taunt the opposite sex and treat each other like objects. From a young age, we must infuse them with *Christ's perspective* on the opposite sex.

Remember Dean and Patti from chapter 5? Their youngest son attends a Christian elementary school. He is already learning to protect femininity. "Preston is the only boy in his class who doesn't tease and make fun of girls," Patti told us. "Since he was very young, we've taught him to see girls the way Christ sees them—as special princesses to be honored and cherished. Even though Preston doesn't especially enjoy spending time around girls yet, he has learned to treat them with kindness and respect. It will be a wonderful foundation for him when he is older."

Dana is the mother of an eleven-year-old girl. "Some of Stacey's friends already flirt with boys and pressure her to do the same," she told us. "But Stacey understands her responsibility to help boys grow into men of honor. And she knows that by flirting with them, she is dishonoring Christ by tempting the boys to lower their standards. So she's chosen not to play the flirting game."

In simple ways such as these, parents can begin helping their young children treat the opposite sex as Christ would.

ACTION PLAN

*Three Practical Ways to Tackle This Challenge
in Your Life Today*

1. **Train boys to honor women.** Help young boys learn how to be gentleman, by practicing on their sisters and mothers. Mark and Julie are the parents of two boys and a girl. Even though their sons are only seven and nine, they are training

them how to honor women. "We take every chance we see to teach our boys how to be gentlemen," Mark says. "They have learned to open doors for their mother. They've learned how to compliment their little sister rather than tear her down. We've taught them that women must be treated with special honor and respect, and we've reinforced that principle in our home. Our boys already see themselves as the protectors of their younger sister."

2. Train girls to honor men. Help young girls learn how to become princesses, by practicing on their dads and brothers. Earlier in this book, we introduced you to Tom and Mary—parents of two girls and a boy between the ages of seven and ten. Even though their daughters are still young, they are training them how to honor men. "We don't allow our girls to speak down to their brother," Mary explains. "We tell them that they have a responsibility to help him grow up into a young prince. Our daughters have learned that the way they treat their brother will have a great effect upon his confidence and masculinity. They've learned to take that responsibility seriously."

3. Help your children practice tenderness in social situations. Don't confine tenderness training to the walls of your home. Social situations are great opportunities for boys to learn how to become gentleman and girls to become graceful princesses. Teach your children how to respect adults, how to treat the opposite sex with kindness instead of ridicule, and how to put others' needs above their own. Not only will they gain an invaluable foundation in the art of tenderness, they will turn a few heads along the way!

MAKING IT PRACTICAL

> ### True-Love Challenge #15
> You want to help your older child develop the art of tenderness.
>
> ### The True-Love Answer
> Utilize your home as the ultimate practice ground for selfless love.

Even when kids are past their most formative seasons, parents can still help train them in the art of tenderness. In college, Eric began to recognize his need to develop the art of tenderness. Yet, he had no idea where to begin. Tenderness was a concept that felt uncomfortable and strange to him.

One day, when his mom was upset about something, he awkwardly approached her and put his arm stiffly on her back. She looked at him quizzically out of the corner of her eye. "I, um," he stammered, "I'm trying to be tender." Instead of rolling her eyes or ridiculing him, Eric's mom recognized a wonderful opportunity to help teach her son the art of tenderness. She fixed his arm around her shoulder, patted it, and said, "There." And over the next few months, Eric's mom became his "tenderness teacher."

"When a woman is crying or emotional," she would tell him, "don't just offer a solution to her problem. Instead, put your arms around her and let her know that you truly care about what she is going through.

"Women like to be taken care of without being asked," she instructed. "Look for little ways to show your love for her by taking the initiative to fill up her car with gas, clean the bathroom, or give her your coat when she is cold."

Eric's mom was a wonderful teacher. As she showed him practical ways to hone the art of tenderness, it became more and more a part of his character. And today in our marriage, I am reaping the benefits of that invaluable training ground!

Similarly, before I was married, my parents helped train me how to be tender toward a man.

"Men like their hard work to be recognized and appreciated," my dad said. "Look at the things that he invests himself into and then notice and compliment those things."

"Instead of nagging a man to get him to do something," my mom told me, "appeal to the heroic protector and leader within him. Tell him you are in need of his unique skills, and then show admiration and appreciation when he offers his help."

As I practiced these tenderness traits on my dad and brothers, I gained a foundation for tenderness in my marriage to Eric.

When parents recognize those invaluable "teachable" moments, they can help young people prepare for a spectacular future romance.

ACTION PLAN

*Two Practical Ways to Tackle This Challenge
in Your Life Today*

1. Teach the differences between men and women. Look for ways to help your children understand the way God has built each of the sexes. Don't expect young men to automatically know how to be sensitive to a woman or young women to intrinsically understand how to be sensitive to a man. Give them direction with simple statements such as, "Women appreciate a man who shows thoughtfulness," or "Men come to life when women notice the things they work hard at." Then, provide them with opportunities to live out those principles, such as pointing out to your son that his mother would really appreciate someone washing her car and filling it with gas, or reminding your daughter that her father has just spent his weekend finishing the deck and could use some gratitude and a glass of lemonade. As you help your older children understand how men and women work and point out practical ways they can show sensitivity to their parents and siblings, they will gain wonderful training for marriage.

2. Help your child recognize opportunities for tenderness. As you seek to direct your older child in the art of tenderness, point out the opportunities that you see in his or her life. If your son is in college, there might be a great practice ground for selflessness in his relationship with his college roommate. If your daughter knows a social outcast, reaching out to that person might provide her with a great practice ground for compassion. As you help open your child's eyes to the opportunities God has given them, you will motivate them to begin training now in the art of true love.

MAKING IT PRACTICAL

True-Love Challenge #16

Your child needs real-life examples of true love in action.

The True-Love Answer

Showcase the art of tenderness in and through your own life.

Even beyond practical training, parents have an amazing opportunity to influence their children toward tenderness simply by setting the right example. When young people personally witness a fleshed-out model of Christlike love, they have a higher standard to aim toward. And when young people witness the wrong example from parents and leaders, they quickly lose a vision for the Christlike model of true love.

I recently heard a young woman repeat a catchy quote she'd heard: "Behind every great man is a woman rolling her eyes." As much as our culture enjoys coming up with those kinds of tidbits, there isn't a bit of truth to statements like that. Men don't become great men when women roll their eyes. They are empowered and ennobled by the *respect* and *honor* of the women in their lives. A woman has a tremendous power to shape a man into a warrior-poet or tear him down into a wimpy wanna-be. It's time we start using that power for good and not harm.

The same is true in reverse. Women don't become great when men mock them and tear them down. They are empowered and ennobled by the *respect* and *honor* of the men in their lives. A man has tremendous power to shape a woman into a Christlike princess or to tear her down into an insecure mess. It's time we start using that power for good and not harm.

ACTION PLAN

Three Practical Ways to Tackle This Challenge
in Your Life Today

1. **Speak only words that honor the opposite sex.** Even if you have been deeply wounded by the words and actions of the opposite sex, don't lead the younger generation on the same path. When parents and leaders begin to speak positively about the opposite sex, we set a healthy pattern in place for the younger generation to model. Make a conscious choice to focus on the positive qualities you see in the members of the opposite sex in your life, and verbalize them on a regular basis.

2. **Show affection to your spouse in front of your children.** When Eric was growing up, his dad did a wonderful job of showing affection to his mom. The very first thing he would do every day when he came home from work was to find his wife and give her a kiss and a hug. Showing physical affection to your spouse might seem like an insignificant thing, but it can have a huge influence upon the younger generation's vision

for marriage. After all, if they see their parents interact only in a cold and distant way, how can they gain a vision of a loving, affectionate marriage?

We often tell the younger generation that physical intimacy is so much more enjoyable and beautiful when they save it until marriage. We tell them that faithfulness to one person for a lifetime is the most fulfilling form of love. But if they observe no physical spark of heat or attraction in their parents' marriage, it doesn't give them much hope that those statements are true.

It isn't necessary to go overboard in showing displays of physical affection in front of your kids. Even a simple hug and kiss everyday will be enough to remind them that marriage and faithfulness isn't dull and boring, but beautiful and fulfilling.

3. Celebrate the blessing of your spouse. One day this week, go out of your way to show appreciation for your spouse in front of your kids. Take a moment at the dinner table, during a prayer, or in the car as a family to verbally reinforce your love and appreciation for your life partner.

In a Nutshell

If your child had a dream of winning an Olympic medal, you wouldn't expect him to start practicing his sport only a few weeks before the Olympic Games. Instead, you would help him devote years of his life to his event. You would wake up before dawn to take them him to practice, you would hire the best coaches and teachers, and you would continually cheer him on as he honed his skill.

Every parent wants their child to win the Olympic gold when it comes to their future marriage. And yet, how many parents actually help their kids train to be the best they can be in this area of their lives? How often do they provide them with the coaching, the discipline, and the encouragement they need to go the distance?

As parents, you have an amazing opportunity to groom the up-and-coming generation in the art of true love, long before they ever meet their future spouse. And there is an incredible practice ground *right in your own home.*

Just think—if young people can learn to be selfless and Christlike in their current family, they will have the right foundation to be selfless and Christlike in their future family. The behavior habit patterns children establish while living at home are the ones that they carry on into their future home. Teach your children the art of tenderness now, helping them practice on you and on their siblings. Then, when they say "I do" they will already possess the foundational tool to make their marriage sparkle and shine for a lifetime. When two people learn to love each other like Christ loved us, laying down their own selfish agendas in order to study and serve one another's needs, they have found the ultimate recipe for true love that stands the test of time.

8

THE LIFELONG PRACTICE OF TRUE-LOVE TRAINING

Becoming a child's lifetime marriage mentor

Leslie

LIFELONG MARRIAGE COUNSELING

JACKSON AND DANA met at a Christian college and became engaged after a few months of dating. Once they set the date for their wedding, their parents suddenly kicked into "counseling mode." Jackson's parents arranged for them to attend five sessions of premarital counseling with their pastor. Dana's mom gave her a handful of Christian marriage books to read.

Like most Christian young people in their generation, Jackson and Dana didn't get much teaching or preparation for marriage during their growing-up years. But in the months leading up to their wedding, Jackson and Dana were put through a crash course on the subject. By the time they walked down the aisle, they at least had a vague grasp of some marriage basics: "Husbands, be understanding toward your wives when they buy a lot of shoes or paint the living room pink. Wives, respect your husbands even when they scream hysterically at the television every Sunday during football season. Learn to love each other even when he leaves the toilet seat up or she spends hours at the mall."

How well equipped are Jackson and Dana for building a strong, healthy, thriving marriage? Is this kind of rushed, shallow preparation really the best head-start for our kids as they ride off into the sunset together?

> If we want today's kids to have the best foundation for marital success, *marriage counseling must begin long before engagement.*

There is *so much more* to the art of marriage than a few basic concepts about women buying shoes or men leaving the toilet seat up. If we want today's kids to have the best foundation for marital success, marriage counseling must begin *long before engagement.* Going through counseling sessions and reading Christian books prior to a wedding are certainly valuable activities, but they can never replace the *lifetime of marriage preparation* that parents are meant to provide for their children.

To have the best foundation for marital success, kids need to grow up with a lifelong understanding of godly marriage. They need to hear words of godly marital wisdom from parents and leaders, even at an early age.

Instead of expecting kids to win the Olympic gold after just a few weeks of practice, let's begin helping them achieve their dream long before the games ever begin.

SETTING "REALISTIC" EXPECTATIONS

Many young adults don't have a realistic view of what their marriage will be. When they meet someone and fall in love, they picture riding off into the sunset together and living happily ever after. But they don't factor in the trials and struggles they will face. They don't envision the challenge of loving another person in the midst of sickness, financial troubles, and family tragedies. They aren't prepared for the intensity of the journey they are headed into. And when the honeymoon ends, many are blindsided with extreme disillusionment and disappointment.

Many Christians address this problem by trying to give young people "realistic" expectations of marriage.

"At some point in your marriage, you will wake up and feel like you married the wrong person," says a Christian marriage counselor. "Don't panic; that's normal. It happens to every married couple."

"You won't always be in love the same way you are on your wedding day," says a Christian marriage-and-family professor. "There will be seasons where you don't feel anything for each other, times when you wish you could go to singles' clubs and meet someone new."

Is this the best approach for a generation already disillusioned with marriage and prone to divorce? Or is there a better way to help young people prepare for the challenges of married love?

Is disillusionment and dissatisfaction just a normal part of the marriage pattern? Do these "realistic" expectations for marriage line up with *God's* expectations for marriage?

In ten years of marriage, Eric and I can honestly say that we have never doubted whether we married the right person. We have never looked across the table at each other and wished we could be with someone else. We have never become disillusioned with our marriage. In fact, it has only grown more beautiful with time. We have only fallen more and more in love as the years have passed.

Has our life been easy? Definitely not. We have faced extreme challenges together over the years. Health problems, financial challenges, and even betrayal from people we trusted are just a few of the struggles we have shared together. Yet, we have clung to each other through times of sorrow and uncertainty. And the trials have only strengthened our love.

Do we have conflict in our marriage? Of course. We work and live together as two imperfect humans! There are plenty of times when we become irritable, impatient, unreasonable, and argumentative, when we take each other for granted or become self-focused and stubborn. But we make it a point to learn and grow from each conflict we face. We don't allow tension to be the norm in our relationship. We don't leave issues unaddressed. We never settle for mediocrity; we always pursue excellence in our relationship. Our marriage is not a perfect fairy tale, but it is a vibrant picture of love that has been deepened and strengthened in the midst of life's challenges.

What is the secret to avoiding marital disillusionment? How can we prepare the next generation to understand the reality of the marriage journey, yet help them strive for excellence instead of mediocrity?

Quite simply: *a Christ-fulfilled existence.* The reason I don't become disillusioned with Eric is that I don't look to him to meet my deepest needs for fulfillment and happiness. The reason he doesn't become discontent with me is that I am not his primary source of security and fulfillment.

Eric and I each have an individual, passionate love relationship with Jesus Christ. And that relationship is our primary source of strength, fulfillment, peace, and happiness. When we draw our strength and security first and foremost from Jesus Christ, we aren't tempted to look to each other to meet the needs that *only He can fulfill.*

Yes, Eric and I meet each other's needs in many ways. Our marriage fulfills our desire for human companionship, physical intimacy, and practical help and support in everyday life. But only Christ can meet our *deepest* longings for unshakable peace, joy, happiness, contentment, and security. Christ alone will never fail us. And Christ must be our first and final source of strength and hope.

That Christ-centered existence is what keeps us from falling prey to the typical marriage disillusionment pattern. Instead of expecting more from Eric than what he can give me, I find my fulfillment in Christ. Then I am free to serve and give to Eric rather than constantly demand from him. And he does the same for me.

Instead of merely telling the younger generation to have "realistic" expectations of marriage, let's begin giving them *God's expectations* for marriage. God wants us to understand and prepare for the intensity and challenge of the marriage journey. But He doesn't want us to settle for disillusionment and mediocrity. He created us for *lifelong marital fulfillment;* a version of marriage that is a foretaste of heaven.

When we teach our children to find their identity and hope

in Christ, rather than looking to an earthly relationship to meet those needs, we offer them a catalyst to a marriage that only grows stronger with time. To become effective marriage mentors, we must give kids realistic expectations for their future—expectations of a Christ-centered, fulfilling romance that grows only stronger throughout the ups and downs of life.

MAKING IT PRACTICAL

True-Love Challenge #17
Your child is growing up in a world in which marriage is under severe attack.

The True-Love Answer
Verbally reinforce God's grand intention for marriage.

Not long ago I attended a wedding shower in which a group of Christian women were giving marriage advice to the bride-to-be.

"When your husband gives you advice, just try not to roll your eyes at him," one of the women said.

"Yes," agreed another. "First turn your back and *then* roll your eyes at him!"

"Try to enjoy the honeymoon season," said a wife of twenty years, "when your husband actually pays attention to you. Because soon reality will set in and he won't even look up from his newspaper anymore."

The comments reminded me of the kind of "advice" I received before Eric and I were married. Other than our parents, nearly every adult in our lives seemed to have incredibly low standards and expectations for what marriage could be.

But in the midst of all the negativity, one married couple who had just celebrated their twenty-fifth anniversary took a different approach. Eric and I have never forgotten their words. "You've probably heard a lot of negative comments about marriage," they told us, "that the romance dies after the honeymoon and all that. But it doesn't have to be that way. We didn't think we could love each other any more than we did on our wedding day. But now, after twenty-five years of marriage, we are so much more in love than we ever were back then. If God is at the center, your marriage will only get more beautiful with time."

If we want the younger generation to experience amazing marriages, we must begin giving them *a vision* for amazing marriages. Young people today see very few examples of really healthy marriages. As parents and leaders, let's begin speaking words of hope and life rather than discouragement and defeat. Let's teach them the sweeter song instead of the world's sour melody.

ACTION PLAN

Three Practical Ways to Tackle This Challenge in Your Life Today

1. Make a conscious choice never to tear down marriage. Your children listen to your words and observe your attitude very closely. Verbally tearing down marriage—even in seemingly harmless ways—can be extremely destructive in their view of what God intends marriage to be. Adopt a godly code of conduct for your words and attitude toward marriage, and don't let anything cause you to lower your guard.

2. Speak only words that honor your spouse. Make a decision never to criticize or tear down your spouse, especially in front of your children. Even if your spouse has plenty of glaring faults, don't point them out. Focus on his or her positive qualities and do everything you can to build up your spouse on a regular basis. As your children hear you speaking words of life toward your spouse, they will gain a godly understanding of what it means to honor their future spouse.

3. Point out Christ-centered relationships. Whether married or single, you can help reinforce the principles of godly marriage by exposing your children to other Christ-centered relationships. Make a list of godly couples in your life and invite each of them over for dinner. Observe little things they do or say that honor each other, and then point those things out to your children after they leave. Make an ongoing effort to help your children be around these godly couples, and encourage them to make their own observations about the strengths they see in those marriages.

Do you see a woman who excels at honoring her husband and praising him in public? Point her out to your children. Do you notice a man who treats his wife with tenderness and consideration? Draw your kids' attention to his example. Do you know a couple who exudes a passionate love for Christ and each other? Point out the godly aspects of their romance. Have you read about an amazing Christ-centered love story? Take some time to share it with your children. The more kids observe glimpses of Christlike love, the more they will know what to aim for in their own future.

MAKING IT PRACTICAL

True-Love Challenge #18
Satan is out to thwart your child's relational future.

The True-Love Answer
Pray daily for your child's future love story.

When my parents first became Christians, I was about two years old. They made a decision to pray for my future husband every single day of my life. They continued this discipline throughout the years, and their prayers became more and more specific. And God answered their prayers in incredible ways. My dad prayed that he and my mother would recognize my future husband when he came into my life—and my parents had a clear sense that Eric was the one for me even before I did. My mom prayed that God would bring a man into my life who loved music as much as I did—and Eric and I developed a friendship because of our mutual love for singing and writing songs, which is something we continue to do together to this day.

As a parent, you have a unique role. You have been appointed by God as the protector and provider of your child's emotional, physical, and spiritual life. When parents take that responsibility seriously and spend time on their knees on behalf of their children, God can do amazing things in and through them.

Even if you haven't been praying for your child's future love story thus far, God will honor your prayers, starting today. The more you pray for your child and her future love story, the more you will gain a clarity and peace about your unique role as her teammate. On your knees you will find the strength and wisdom to offer the support, encouragement, advice, correction, discipline, and help your child needs to discover God's very best.

ACTION PLAN

Two Practical Ways to Tackle This Challenge
in Your Life Today

1. Plan a daily time for consistent prayer. Tape a reminder note to your bedpost, bathroom mirror, or refrigerator to remind you to pray for this area of your child's life until it becomes habitual. Every day when you do a certain activity, such as brush your teeth, pour your coffee, or get into bed, offer up a prayer for your child's future love story.

2. Write down a list of specific prayers. As God gives you specific desires and dreams for your child's future love story, write them down and commit them to regular prayer. Let God shape your prayers into more mature and specific requests as the years go by. Keep a journal of how you see God working in your child's life, and record all the displays of His faithfulness you observe along the way. Consider sharing your years of thoughts, prayers, and observations with your child and his or her spouse as a special wedding or engagement present.

In a Nutshell

There is so much more to the art of marriage than a few basic concepts about women buying shoes or men leaving the toilet seat up. If we want our children to have the best foundation for marital success, marriage counseling must begin *long before engagement*. Going through counseling sessions and reading Christian books prior to a wedding are certainly valuable activities, but they can never replace the *lifetime of marriage preparation* that you as a parent are meant to provide for your children.

To have the best foundation for marital success, your kids need to grow up with a deeper understanding of what marriage is meant to be. They need to be taught principles for selflessness and faithfulness. They need to hear words of godly marital wisdom from parents and leaders, even at an early age.

Instead of merely telling the younger generation to have "realistic" expectations of marriage, let's begin giving them *God's expectations* for marriage. God wants us to understand and prepare for the intensity and challenges of the marriage journey. But He doesn't want us to settle for disillusionment and mediocrity. He created us for *lifelong marital fulfillment;* a version of marriage that is a foretaste of heaven. Let's begin helping kids train for the Olympic gold in marriage, starting today.

Part Five

BEYOND LOVE STORIES

We have a God who delights in impossibilities and who asks, "Is anything too hard for Me?"
—ANDREW MURRAY

The greatest Old or New Testament saints who ever lived were at a level that is quite within our reach. The same spiritual power that enabled them to become our spiritual heroes is also available to us.
—EDWARD MYRICK GOULBURN

The mark of a life governed by the Holy Spirit is that such a life is continually and ever more and more occupied with Christ, that Christ becomes greater and greater as time goes on.
—T. AUSTIN-SPARKS

Epilogue
SHOULDERS OF GIANTS

> *Providing a heavenly foundation upon which today's young people can build*

Leslie
BECOMING ONE OF THE FEW

AMY CARMICHAEL, A PIONEER of mission work in India, chose a set-apart life at the age of seventeen. "The preoccupations of seventeen-year-old girls—their looks, their clothes, their social life—don't change much from generation to generation," wrote Elisabeth Elliot in Amy's biography. "But in every generation there seem to be a few who make other choices. Amy was one of the few."[1]

In today's sex-at-thirteen generation, there are young people, like Amy Carmichael, who are making other choices. They are the set apart. They are the few. They are those who encounter the God of the universe and allow Him to radically shape every aspect of their lives. They are those who, as Bishop Bardsley wrote, "care not at all what the world thinks of them, because they are entirely taken up with the tremendous reality of God."[2]

But these set-apart ones need not be found only among the younger generation. What about *your* life? What about *your* generation? As a parent or leader, are you willing to become one of the few in *your* generation who makes different choices? Rather than merely cheering your kids on from the sidelines, you have the opportunity to become a spiritual pioneer for future generations to follow. Not many parents are willing to rise to the challenge. Will you be among the few who are?

It's so easy to compare ourselves to those around us. Maybe we are a few steps ahead of the culture when it comes to raising our children, training them in purity, and teaching them about God's ways. Maybe our marriage is better than most others we see. But instead of walking a few steps beyond the culture and then pitching our tent, God calls us to so much more. He calls us to a lifetime of pursuing Him, learning of Him, growing in Him, and being made into His likeness. He calls us to follow Him into an endless frontier—a lifetime of discovery, a lifelong adventure of His power at work in our lives.

When Eric and I ask the younger generation to list their spiritual heroes—the people in their lives who have most inspired them to pursue Jesus Christ—very few of them name their parents. Though they might love and respect their mom and dad, few young people would describe their parents as heroic spiritual pioneers who constantly propel them forward into a boundless adventure with God. Today's Christian parents are generally regarded by young people as "comfortable Christians," those who do the spiritual basics and then settle down in the land of the predictable.

The younger generation is hungry for a passionate adventure with God. They are ready to pour their lives out to Him with abandon, to become the few in their generation to live lives that make an eternal impact upon this world. They are longing for "fathers and mothers of the faith," those who have gone before them and made a map for them to follow into God's endless frontier. Yet many never find what they seek. They want to stand on the shoulders of giants, but they see no spiritual giants upon which to stand.

The younger generation needs parents who don't just teach them the right things but whose lives are an inspiring, radiant reflection of Jesus Christ. They need heroes to look up to, spiritual leaders to follow.

What would happen to today's younger generation if a *new generation* of parents emerged—parents who became spiritual pioneers instead of spiritual settlers, parents who rose above the mediocrity of the culture, and parents who led their children into the endless frontier of God's ways?

We would begin to see not merely a few set-apart young people in the midst of a perverse culture, but an entire generation of young people who grow up understanding what it means to give their lives wholly and completely to Jesus Christ. We would begin to see change that lasts for generations to come.

In every parental generation, there are a few who rise above the settlers' mindset, who reject the pattern of the culture, and who lead their children into God's endless frontier. Are you willing to be one of the few?

❈

Catherine Booth was a mother of eight who lived in the 1800s. From a young age, she felt that God had called her to become a "mother of nations." She devoted every aspect of her life to serving her Lord. Even though she was afflicted with many painful ailments throughout her life, she drew strength, grace, and supernatural joy from her intimate, daily walk with Christ.

Tirelessly, she worked alongside her husband William, serving the poor and spreading the gospel to the unsaved. She was passionate about calling Christians out of spiritual mediocrity into a vibrant relationship with God, and soon she became one of the most well-known female evangelists in her country. William and Catherine's powerful ministry of revival and evangelism began to spread around the world.

Yet even as Catherine poured out her life for others and traveled to other nations, she never neglected her children. She dedicated each of her eight children from infancy to service for God. Her desire and goal was to build a family of warriors for Christ. Throughout their lives she counseled them and watched over their spiritual development, education, and relationships. "We are made for larger ends than earth can compass," she constantly exhorted her children. "Oh let us be true to our exalted destiny."

Catherine's radiant spiritual life and passionate pursuit of Christ became a map that led her children into God's endless frontier. Every one of her children wholeheartedly devoted their lives to Jesus Christ. Her eight sons and daughters—as well as all of her sons-in-law and daughters-in-law—gave their lives to the service of God's kingdom, many of them working alongside Catherine and William in their ministry. It was written of the Booths that "no family in recent Christian history has served the poor and the outcast, the prisoner and the hoodlum so diligently, bringing them to the healing ministry of Christ. They went forth to distant corners of the globe."

Catherine watched her children set out on difficult missions, facing persecution and mockery for their faith and ministry. And yet she did not seek to coddle or shelter them from trials, but encouraged them to spill out their lives for Christ, to sacrifice everything they had for Him no matter what the cost.

"Rise up on the strength of God and resolve to conquer," she wrote to one of her daughters who was facing a spiritual challenge. "My love for you makes me desire God's highest good for your life. How can love desire less? Anything that desires less is selfishness, not love."

So profound was Catherine's spiritual impact upon the lives of her children that two of her sons-in-law adopted the Booth name as part of their own. One of them compiled a two-volume biography of the life of his mother-in-law.

When Catherine became terminally ill at the age of sixty, fifty-thousand people gathered to hear her last message. And when she died a short time later, fifty thousand people once more gathered for her funeral, filing past her casket and mourning her loss for five days. Her husband praised her as the one who had "understood the rise and fall of his feelings, the bent of his thoughts, and the purpose of his existence." Her children praised her as the one who had "nurtured and trained them for the service of the living God."

Catherine was one of the few mothers in her generation who chose a truly set-apart life. And as a result she left a spiritual legacy for her children and her children's children to follow. [3]

❖

Susannah Wesley had a difficult life. A beautiful and intelligent woman who lived in the late 1600s, she married a poor curate who was burdened by debt and severe financial difficulties. She gave birth to nineteen children, but only nine lived to adulthood. She raised her family amid poverty, sickness, and countless trials, yet she never lost hope in God.

In spite of her countless responsibilities as a wife, mother, and teacher, she withdrew to her room each day to spend two hours in God's presence, seeking Him, listening to Him, and pouring out her heart to Him. It was this intimate relationship with her Lord that transformed her life from one of failure into eternal victory.

Year after year, she poured herself out for her children, teaching them the ways of God. Their spiritual welfare was what mattered most to her. "Grant me grace, Lord, to be wholly a Christian," was her constant prayer. "Let me not confine my faith to the church or closet, prayer or meditation, but to remain in Your presence everywhere I am."

Six hours a day for twenty years, she patiently educated her children—so thoroughly that they became passionate for learning and righteousness. She called her children to rise above the standards of the culture. "Do not live like the rest of mankind," she told them, "who pass through the world like straws upon a river, carried whichever way the stream or wind drive them. Instead live in the constant presence of the great and holy God. He is about our beds and about our paths and sees all our ways. Whenever you are tempted to give way to sin, pause and say to yourself, 'What am I about to do? God sees me.'"

All of her children devoted their lives to Christ. Her sons Charles and John Wesley became two of the greatest spiritual reformers of their generation. The men attributed much of their spiritual success to the influence of their mother. When John became a noted man, he asked his mother to write down the details of her education of her children. Susannah reluctantly agreed but feared that many would not understand what she had done with her life. "No one can, without renouncing the world in the most literal sense, observe my method," she said. "There are few, if any, who would devote twenty years of the prime of life in hopes to save the souls of their children."

But Susannah Wesley had done just that. Even when Charles and John became men of great influence, with thousands clamoring to hear their passionate preaching, they continued to seek the counsel and wisdom of their beloved mother.

Susannah was one of the few mothers in her generation who chose a truly set-apart life. And as a result she left a spiritual legacy for her children and her children's children to follow.[4]

❖

James Paton was a poor Scottish peasant in the 1800s. At seventeen, he gave his life fully to Jesus Christ. He was passionate and devoted to his Lord, spending hours in prayer and the study of God's ways. His greatest desire was to become a minister of the gospel; to take the truth of Christ to the unsaved of the world. But James's life circumstances and financial hardships continued to prevent this from being possible, until finally he began to accept that God had a different plan for his life. He was married at an early age and vowed that if God gave him sons, he would consecrate them unreservedly to the ministry of

Christ. Though peasants could not easily become missionaries, James trusted that God would somehow open up a way for his children to take the gospel to the unsaved, if it was His will.

James and his wife had eleven children. James took his responsibility as a father as seriously as if he had been sent on a holy mission of God. Tirelessly guiding his family in prayer, worship, discipline, and a deep understanding of God, he set a spiritual standard that inspired and motivated his children to give their lives completely to Jesus Christ. He made a map for his children to follow into God's endless frontier.

John, James's oldest son, once described the profound effect of his father's spiritual influence upon his life. "How much my father's prayers impressed me I can never explain, nor could any stranger understand," he wrote. "On his knees with all of us kneeling around him in family worship, he poured out his whole soul with tears for the conversion of the heathen world, and for every personal and domestic need. We all felt as if we were in the presence of the living Savior, and learned to know and love Him as our Divine Friend. As we rose from our knees I used to look at the light on my father's face, and wish I were like him in spirit—hoping that, in answer to his prayers, I might be privileged and prepared to carry the blessed gospel to some portion of the heathen world."

The impact of such a devoted follower of Christ upon the life of his son made an eternal difference in countless lives. Miraculously, God open a door for John to enter the ministry as a young man. At thirty-three he sailed to the New Hebrides Islands in the South Pacific to pour out his life among the tribal people there—cannibals who had never seen a white person.

On the day John set out from his home to begin his ministry training, his father walked with him the first six miles of his journey. "My father's counsels and tears and heavenly conversation on that parting journey are fresh in my heart as if it had been but yesterday," wrote John years later. "For the last half-mile we walked in unbroken silence. My father's lips kept moving in silent prayers for me, and his tears fell fast when our eyes met each other in looks for which all speech was vain. We halted on reaching the appointed parting place. He grasped my hand firmly and said, 'God bless you, my son! Your father's God prosper you and keep you from all evil!' Unable to say more, his lips kept moving in silent prayer. In tears we embraced, and parted.

"I ran off as fast as I could, and when about to turn a corner in the road where he would lose sight of me, I looked back and saw him still standing where I had left him, gazing after me. Waving my hat in farewell, I was round the corner and out of sight. But my heart was too full and sore to carry me further, so I darted into the side of the road and wept for a time. Then, rising up cautiously, I climbed the dyke to see if he yet stood where I had left him, and at that moment I caught a glimpse of him climbing the dyke and looking out for me. He did not see me, and after he had gazed eagerly in my direction for a while he got down, began to return home—his heart, I felt sure, still rising in prayers for me. I watched through blinding tears till his form faded from my gaze. Then hastening on my way, I vowed deeply, by the help of God, to live and act so as never to grieve or dishonor such a father as He had given me.

"The appearance of my father when we parted that day— his advice, prayers, and tears—have often, all through my life, risen vividly before my mind. In my earlier years particularly, when exposed to many temptations, his parting form rose before me as that of a guardian angel. It is deep gratitude, which makes me testify here that the memory of that scene not only helped, by God's grace, to keep me pure from the prevailing sins, but also stimulated me in all my studies that I might not fall short of his hopes, and in all my Christian duties that I might faithfully follow his shining example."

James's fervent prayers and shining example to his son was not in vain. John Paton became one of the most influential missionaries of all time, led thousands to the knowledge of Christ and is considered to be among the fifty greatest foreign missionaries in the Victorian age.

James Paton was one of the few fathers in his generation who chose a truly set-apart life. And as a result he left a spiritual legacy for his children and his children's children to follow. [5]

✤

Young people are longing for "fathers and mothers of the faith" like these, spiritual heroes they can look up to and strive to emulate. When just *one parent* is willing to embrace the sacred call of God upon their life and boldly lead his or her children into God's endless frontier, the course of history can be changed forever.

Our children are growing up amid a perverse and declining generation. Yet hope is far from lost. Through your prayers, passion for Christ, and shining spiritual example, you can make a map for your children to follow into a new frontier— God's frontier. Your life can become the catalyst that helps them rise above the slime of the culture and pursue the amazing adventure of a Christ-built life. You can become the instrument that transforms a sex-at-thirteen generation into a set-apart generation.

As C. T. Studd, the famous missionary to Africa, lay dying, he surveyed the tiny hut in which he lay, gazing on his paltry earthly possessions. "I wish I had something to leave to each of you," he stated weakly to the small group gathered about his cot, "but I gave it all to Jesus long ago."[6] Such are the final words of a heroic parent; a parent who does not merely leave an earthly legacy for his children, but a legacy that will last for all eternity.

Who will be the C. T. Studds, the Catherine Booths, the Susannah Wesleys, and the James Patons of today's parental generation? Could it be you?

Bonus Section
HELPING KIDS LIVE HEROIC LIVES

Beyond great love stories . . . into great life stories.

Eric

I'LL NEVER FORGET MY DAD'S VOICE on the phone that day.

I was twenty-three and well on my way in the world. Time and again, I had told myself that my dad's words to me couldn't possibly be *that* important. I hadn't heard him say the words, "I love you, Son," for over twelve years at that point in my life. But I was still alive and kicking, still a confident and generally successful young man. I knew he loved me. Why did I care if he actually said the words? I mean, how much impact can the words, "I love you, Son," really have anyway?

That day on the phone, I found out.

"Uh, Eric?" his voice was full of emotion. I was taken aback. My dad's voice *never* betrayed emotion. This was definitely a first. "I know I haven't done a good job in expressing myself to you over the years, and I'm sorry for that," he said. "But I want you to know now that . . . *I love you, Son.*"

There have been many moments in my life when I have established mental memorials—memorials intended to mark important and significant occasions in my existence. At the malleable age of twenty-three, this phone conversation with my dad was one such moment.

"I love you, Son!" These are simple words, yet words that have given me wings.

When I was twenty-three, my dad began to awaken to the formative power of his words in my life. Since that unforgettable moment on the phone that day, there have been many times when he has spoken the words of life that I desperately needed to hear. "Eric, have I ever told you that I'm proud of you?" or "Eric, I see you as a man!"

My parents' life-giving words have infused me with confidence. They have given me the strength to pursue God's best for my life. They have parted the waters of the Jordan and allowed me to cross over to the other side.

But my parents haven't invested into my life with words alone. They back up their words with a life poured out for their children.

Leslie and I had been laboring in ministry for approximately three years when I received another significant call from my dad. We were suffocating beneath the weight of the growth, the expectation, and the pressure. We were carrying a load that, as a young newly married couple, we were physically unable to carry and spiritually not yet mature enough to know how to yield fully to God.

"Eric," my dad's voice was determined and confident, "I've quit my job, and I am coming to work with you and Leslie. God has given you a message, and as your dad, I'm making myself available to you and to God to enable you to continue sharing it!"

My dad left everything he knew to enter a world he knew nothing about. For a period of five years, my dad's full-time job, no matter how much Leslie and I may have attempted to persuade him otherwise, was simply to wash our feet and lift our arms up during the battle. My dad left himself on the field for me. He didn't just take his job as father to mean keeping me well fed throughout my growing-up years and then helping me get into a good college program. He understood it to mean that he must do whatever it takes for me to find the fulfillment of Christ's purpose in my life.

WHAT MAKES A GOOD PARENT *GREAT*

Leslie and I didn't realize what we were getting into when we stepped into a life of full-time ministry. We picked up a baseball bat (theoretically speaking), swung it straight into a hornets' nest, and only then realized that our feet were cast in concrete. During our ten years of ministry, God has allowed us to be buffeted with extraordinary challenges—challenges that often seemed impossible to burden.

In the midst of one such impossible challenge, I sat in a rental car with my dad outside a Wendy's in Sacramento, California. Just minutes earlier, my dad had informed me that a man we had trusted in our ministry had betrayed us and run off with the ministry's money. We had nothing! Bills were due, salary checks needed to be written, and our ministry didn't have a dime to its name. My dad and I just sat in the car, silent, staring forlornly out the through the car window. I was desperately trying to lean on God, to trust Him completely, but the ache over the betrayal and the frustration with the endless cycle of struggles that kept hitting us was overwhelming me. I needed a voice of reason, a voice of strength. It was in this morass of confusion that my dad spoke to me.

"Eric," he said, turning and looking me in the eye, "God makes His men strong through such trials. He has a great purpose for your life, and this is not the end!" Then with a look of fierce love and fiery resolve that I will never forget, he added, "And Eric, even if you go down, I want you to know that I will go down with you!"

Good parents become *great* parents when they know how to penetrate the life of their kids with heroic vision. Great parents learn to say simple words of truth when those words are most needed. They learn to forsake all to help their children reach beyond them and take the truth of Christ to this world.

My parents were great parents. They planted the seeds within me for something more than mediocrity. They inspired me to passionately seek after my God, and then they helped me learn how to do it. They trained me for a version of confidence profoundly more effective than self-confidence—they taught me to trust the Almighty God of the universe implicitly and wholly. They taught me Christ-confidence! They built me to be a communicator with my life, not one who hides the light of the gospel, but one who stands upon a high hill and shines His light for the world to see.

Heroic kids are the result of heroic parents. By that I don't mean parents who are perfect, but parents who won't ever stop growing, learning, and following God further into His endless frontier of His love, power, and grace.

My dad's dad didn't set for him an example of speaking life-building and character-inspiring words to his children. Words like "I love you, Son" were a foreign concept to my dad in the context of a father-son relationship when I was growing up.

When I was a young boy, my dad told me he loved me and kissed me every night as he tucked me into bed. But as I grew into my teen years, it became uncomfortable and awkward to say such things and to express his affection to me in that way.

Yet when my dad learned how truly important it was for me that he begin speaking life-building and character-inspiring words to me as a young man, *he began speaking them,* no matter how uncomfortable he felt in doing it. Heroic parents are willing to do whatever it takes to see the work of God progress in their child's life, even if it means extreme discomfort for them.

Unfortunately, there are only a few parents in each generation who resolve to give more to their kids than what is deemed socially necessary. There are only a handful of parents in every ten thousand who are willing to get uncomfortable to enable their kids' spiritual success. But the parents who produce the heroic world changers are those who heroically give of themselves in the battle for their child's soul.

In this bonus section, it is our hope to take the message of this book one step further—beyond love stories and into the realm of life stories. We want to briefly explore the familial building blocks of world changers and discuss how you as a parent can help instill a sense of the heroic into your children from a young age. From the vantage point of a child, great parenting isn't complicated stuff—it's simply being willing to leave it all on the field to see them succeed. And it's not always big things that are necessary. Sometimes it's things as small as the words, "I love you, Son," that inspire a young life to move from the mediocre domain into the magnanimous one. But, as parents, you'll never know until you try.

HEROIC PARENTING GOAL #1

Raising Up Real-life Super-Heroes

As a parent, you choose the destination for your children—the desert of mediocrity or the land of the extraordinary! You define the possibilities of their lives. You are the one who tells them if they are built for small things or if they are capable of changing the world. It's your words that form their perception of themselves. You choose for them either *the desert* or *the dream land*.

When we read about the Israelites in the Old Testament stuck in the wilderness, we often don't think of our own lives being very similar to theirs. After all, they lived thousands of years ago and their story took place on the opposite end of the globe. However, just like the Israelites from way back when, we as Christians must decide where we will set up spiritual camp—*the desert* or *the dream land*. The choice is ours!

The Israelites chose to set up camp in the miserable desert, even though that wasn't where God wanted them to pitch their tents. In effect, God had simply said, "Trust Me, and I will give you a land over yonder that flows with milk and honey." And still, a vast majority of the Israelites chose to pitch their tents in the wilderness instead. What was wrong with these people?

Were they crazy? Why choose mediocrity when you could choose extraordinary?

The answer is—*the ease factor.* And it's the very same ease factor that causes countless modern Christian parents today to raise their kids in the wilderness of mediocrity rather than the promised land of the extraordinary.

After all, the mediocre life doesn't require anything of us but a few basic, easily defined daily tasks. The mediocre life relies on human ability and doesn't have to worry about taking God into account and giving Him the pen. The mediocre life produces your everyday, average kid who grows up to be your-everyday, average adult. And there's nothing wrong with average, is there?

But what if God has so much more in mind for us?

The extraordinary life requires *everything:* every facet of our being, every ounce of our strength, and every moment of our day. The extraordinary life relies on God's ability, not human strength. It spends itself wholly and completely on His agenda. And while the extraordinary life doesn't score well on the ease factor scale, it does produce superheroic kids who dream God-sized dreams and see God-sized results throughout their entire lives.

The Israelite leaders sent twelve spies into the Promised Land to survey their enemy. On their return, only two of the spies actually believed God was big enough to defeat the huge giants and enemy armies in the land. The other ten were so impressed with the size of their opposition that they concluded God couldn't possibly overcome, that He must have meant for them to stay in the desert.

Often, when it comes to our lives, to our marriages, and to

our kids, all we see are the obstacles, and the impossibilities, rather than the God of the impossible. We often have more faith in the power of our obstacles than we do in the God of the universe to overcome our obstacles.

Christian superheroes are made *first in their mentality* and *then with their actions.* Heroic young people are shaped first through their parents' heroic vision for their life and then through trusting God to make it all possible. The people who enter the Promised Land are those who trust God to be as big as He says He is and allow Him to work the miraculous on their behalf. They are those who chuckle at the size of enemy giants, because they are so taken up with the enormity of their huge God.

There are many reasons that countless Christians choose to pass their days in the wilderness. It's just plain easier, for one thing. No one fights you when you are in the desert. All the great evil armies hanging out in Canaan don't mind your pitching your tent in the middle of nowhere, they only care that you stay out of *their* territory. And everything is predictable in the desert—you've got your cloud by day and pillar of fire by night and you have your manna deposited from heaven every morning. It's all routine in the wilderness! *It's the life on the far side of the Jordan that poses the difficulties.* The great battle will commence in our lives when we finally allow God to be as big as He says He is and take us across the Jordan into the hostile territory. That is where great lives are lived.

So how can you raise your kids to be pioneers rather than settlers? How can you inspire them to be God trusters rather than wilderness wanderers? How can you train them to fix their gaze on their huge God rather than their formidable enemies? An endless frontier of Promised Land awaits every child of God. Your children are loaded with the potential to experience an extraordinary life right along with every historic Christian who has ever walked this globe. But you play an important role in making that happen.

Start by thinking bigger yourself. You must shift your gaze first before your kids will know to shift theirs. If you are pitching your tent in the wilderness, it doesn't necessarily mean that your child is destined to do the same, but it does mean that she probably doesn't even realize that there is opportunity for something so much better out there. When you begin to talk about the Promised Land of God (the plan of God for each of our lives) with your children, then your children begin to awaken to the possibilities of this great God-crafted adventure. It stirs within them a longing to go there, to see it, to experience it for themselves.

My mom and dad used to frequently say to me, "Eric, God has great things in store for your life!" Those words were always grand and richly laden with possibility. "Eric, there is no limit to what God can do in and through your life if you fully yield to Him!" Words of truth like these inspired me to dream big dreams and to pursue a superhero existence with God.

Through my parents' words and example, I was introduced to a heroic God who built heroic men. He was a God without limit, without end. He never ran out of frontier for His explorers to venture into. He never gave a final resting spot for spiritual pioneers to pitch their tent.

Yes, it's dangerous to dream God-sized dreams. If we simply live in the predictable and the comfortable, we can pass our days without disruption . . . and without consequence. But

God trains his children to live grandiose lives that wholly lean the weight of their existence upon His faithfulness. Young people who learn to dream God's dreams find themselves taking God-sized risks, and often experience surprising degrees of difficulty in their lives. Yet they fully live, and the impact of their lives lasts for generations after them.

In our book, *When God Writes Your Life Story*, Leslie and I give our generation the ingredients necessary to a superheroic life. We introduce them to God's Mt. Everest expectations for their existence; we introduce them to the Promised Land.

And just like the Israelites surveying the Promise Land thousands of years ago, we realize how comically impossible it is to go there! The desert, though dull and mundane, is at least reasonable and safe. The Promised Land on the other hand is loaded with challenges and insurmountable obstacles. What God has called each of His children to is humanly impossible. But God doesn't have a smirk on his face when He beckons us to follow Him across the Jordan and into the land full of enemy giants. *He's not joking.* He means what He says. He wants us to trust that He is fully capable of working the impossible in and through our lives. He beckons us simply to allow Him to be as big as He says He is.

It's a simple fact—God has bigger dreams for your children than do you. *He didn't design them for the desert—He built them for the dream land!* He wants your child, like the heroes of old, to "shut the mouths of lions, quench the furious blaze of fire, escape the edge of the sword, have his weakness turned to strength, and become powerful in battle—routing foreign armies" (see Hebrews 11:33–34).

What He has in mind for your child may seem utterly

impossible to you. But to become a heroic parent, you must absorb the reality that our God is the God of the impossible. He deliberately takes His children through impossible waters to prove Himself as the God of insurmountable odds, and as a result they came become official spokesmen and women for a life full of faith and superheroism.

HEROIC PARENTING GOAL #2

Inspiring Passionate Christ-Lovers

"Study your Bible," parents and leaders often say to young people. "Pray, worship, and learn about God." Often young Christians know *what* they are supposed to be doing in their spiritual lives, but they have no idea *how* to do any of those things.

When it comes to studying their Bible, they flop it open and stare at the page hoping that by looking at the text it will somehow supernaturally deposit itself within their souls. Prayer becomes a ritual of saying the same things over and over. Worship becomes the mindless singing of songs with arms raised. It's not for lack of sincerity that they miss the real point of these spiritual arts. *It is merely lack of training.*

Cultivating intimacy with Christ is similar to cultivating intimacy in marriage. A vibrant marriage doesn't just happen, it requires focused time and effort. A vibrant relationship with Christ is no different. Heroic parents know how to train kids in the art of knowing Christ—not just head knowledge about Him, but *heart* knowledge that comes through time spent in

His presence. Training kids how to build their lives around intimacy with Christ is the most important job a parent can tackle; *it is the key to success in every area of a young person's existence.*

So let's get practical. How can we train our children to pursue a passionate personal relationship with the King of all kings?

In my marriage there are four tools that help my intimate relationship with Leslie to grow. These same four tools are what every young Christian can use to cultivate an intimate love relationship with Christ.

Tool #1

I study my wife. That may sound strange, but it's true. The way some people study business law or the stock market, I study Leslie. I watch her, listen to her, and attempt to understand how she thinks. I seek to know her desires, expectations, and concerns. I labor to be the world's foremost expert on her life, so that I can be the world's greatest servant to her purpose here on earth. It's not hard, but it takes a determined effort. I keep a journal of my observations, and I write down the things that I observe in her and the things that I see God desiring to do in and through her life. And as a result, I know her better than anyone else, and she feels known and understood. She trusts me with the deepest parts of her being and allows me to share in her most intimate thoughts. I know how to serve her because I know who she really is and what she really needs.

The Christ application: Many of us approach Christ as if He is an academic subject rather than a real person. But just like Leslie, He desires to be studied, watched, and listened to. He wants us to intimately understand His desires, expectations, and concerns. He wants us to labor to be the world's foremost expert on His life so that we can become heaven's greatest servant to His purpose here on earth. Just as Leslie gives herself fully to me when she realizes that I am eager to know her, so our God loves to reveal Himself to us when we simply begin our passionate pursuit. When we pursue Him with all our heart and learn to cherish His ways, He shares His intimate thoughts with us more and more.

Since I can physically interact with Leslie, it's easy to see how I can study her, watch her, listen to her, and understand her. But how does one do that with God? That's where the Bible comes in. When a young person is taught to approach the Bible as a means of studying and knowing the great God of the universe, it makes a whole lot more sense from the word "go." The Bible contains the thoughts of God, the desires of God, the purposes of God, and the nature of God. We can understand Him and serve Him, by devouring His very words written to us and for us. The study of Scripture is more than just a "flopping open" of that sacred book. It's an art form motivated out of a passionate longing to know and serve. Let's begin teaching young people how to *explore* their Bible—how to dig deep into God's word and learn of their Lord. A wonderful place to start is by doing an inductive Bible study with your child and helping him or her learn how to allow Scripture to come alive. (Some great resources can be found at www.precept.org and in Howard Hendricks's *Living by the Book*.)

Tool #2

I remember my wife. In other words, I take time to meditate on her life and on her unique qualities. In romance and friendship, this is called thoughtfulness. It goes beyond merely studying Leslie into actually *fleshing out* what I have learned about her. Studying Leslie may reveal to me that she could really use encouragement. But *remembering* her may mean writing out a list of everything I appreciate about her life and pondering ways to share those things with her. Remembrance is a way of holding on to what I study, taking it further, and growing deeper in my relationship with Leslie.

The Christ application: Taking time to remember and meditate upon what we have learned about our God is one of the number one ways to cultivate a profound affection for Him within our souls. In historic Christianity, the art of meditation on Christ was what Christians used to prepare them to worship God. They spent time in deep reflection of His truth and His divine person. Then, worship came naturally. They couldn't possibly hold back their tongues from crying out in adoration and praise. To spend time with God is supposed to be so much more than just passing time in silence. It's an exercise of the soul, basking in His love and truth and being stirred afresh to express our devotion to Him in every area of our lives. Let's begin teaching young people how to remember their God— how to dwell on the truth they have learned about Him until it becomes a part of who they are. Carve out time in your child's schedule for meditating on truth; teach him how to immerse his heart and mind in the amazing reality of God.

Tool #3

I honor my wife with my words. I study Leslie, then I meditate upon her, but not so that I can keep all those thoughts and affections to myself. I study her and remember her so that I can give to her, honor her, and fully appreciate her life. When I spend an hour thinking about all the things I appreciate about her, those thoughts then begin to flow into a hundred different forms of creative expression. I may write her a love note, a love song, a love poem, or even give her a loving touch. The purpose of study and reflection is to build a relationship, not just gain head knowledge. When Leslie finds a love note taped to her mirror in the bathroom when she wakes up in the morning, it stirs her heart and draws her closer to me. She loves to hear my words when they are spoken out of my time spent remembering her. My words are her great personal treasures.

The Christ application: So many of us arrive at church on a Sunday morning with sleep in our eyes and grog in our throats, and begin singing love songs to God. We assume He doesn't care how we sing to Him; we just think that He finds some kind of pleasure in hearing us sing truthful things about Him. But God *does* care how we worship Him. He doesn't just want us to belt out truthful sayings into the universe. God loves the very same thing that Leslie loves—*genuine* adoration and apprecia-tion. He wants us to mean the things we say to Him, to feel them, have them stir so intensely within our souls that we can't help but belt them out. He doesn't want hollow words expressed with hands raised; He simply wants us to know Him, remember Him, and then because of the overwhelming affection within our hearts, to write Him love notes, sing Him love songs, and scrawl Him love poems *with our very lives.*

Let's begin teaching young people how to *truly worship* their God—how to let their praise and adoration flow from the time they have spent dwelling on His truth and basking in

His presence. Worship isn't just singing songs on Sunday mornings. *It is a life lived to honor the God that we love with all our hearts.* Earlier in this book, we shared the story of James Paton—a devoted Christian father who made it his life's pursuit to teach his children the ways of God. His son described the impact of his father's training his family in the art of worship: "On his knees with all of us kneeling around him in family worship, he poured out his whole soul with tears for the conversion of the heathen world, and for every personal and domestic need. We all felt as if we were in the presence of the living Savior, and learned to know and love Him as our Divine Friend."[1] Let James's example be your guide. Teach your children to understand the art of heartfelt worship.

Tool #4

I share my entire life with Leslie. I share a home with her, a bed with her, my dreams with her. I abide with her, in the truest sense of the word. I spend my life attuned to her, being available to her, enjoying her, and loving her. If there is ever something that she needs, all she must do is ask. She always has access to my life, and though I may be occupied doing a thousand different things, I am always available to serve her if she has any need, small or great. Sharing my life with Leslie takes on many forms, but all of them are simply an expression of my given-ness to her. At times we share our thoughts, at times we share our concerns or complaints, at times we make requests of one another, at times we simply speak words of encouragement and grace, and then there are even times when we say nothing but remain in stillness cherishing each other's life. Sharing life together is the ultimate purpose for our relationship.

The Christ application: To share our entire life with Christ is the essence of prayer. Prayer means communing with Him, sharing our thoughts, our concerns, our requests, and our words of praise. This is what prayer is all about. It's a sharing of life. It's not the repetition of certain words over and over again. It's the giving of oneself, constantly attuned to God, constantly available, and constantly willing. Sometimes we commune in stillness, sometimes we speak, and sometimes we sing. But it's all a form of prayer. Christ said, "Abide in me" (John 15:4 NASB). He asks us to offer Him our entire existence and allow Him to make our body His home. Let's begin teaching young people how to *share their lives with* God—to abide in Him. Encourage them to commune with Him throughout the day, to yield to His gentle voice of guidance and direction. Cultivate time in your child's life for regular times of prayer—whether writing in a prayer journal or simply pouring out his thoughts to Him inwardly. Train him how to walk through life *with* Christ, not just representing Him, but enjoying Him. He longs to become the center of your child's existence.

❖

The Christian life isn't a list of rules to follow, but a great God to pursue and know. Let's not just point our kids in the direction of God, but teach them how to find Him, to experientially know Him and love Him. The kids who *know* God are the kids who can *fully trust* God.

Where are your kids headed? Are they aimed toward the

desert or into the *dream land?* If you desire the dream land for your child, then begin acquainting her with the God that can get her there. When God truly overtakes a young person's life, parents no longer need to worry about "keeping her on the right track" in relationships or life direction. If God is a young person's entire focus and passion, all the other pieces of her life will fall supernaturally into place.

HEROIC PARENTING GOAL #3

Crafting Christ-Confident Kids

Still to this day, I consider it to be one of the most significant moments of my life. I remember sitting in my parents' bedroom with my dad and mom. I had no idea what to expect. My dad was different than I had ever seen him. His typical stature and strength seemed to have melted away, replaced with a quiet hum of humility and softness.

"Well, Eric," he began in a halting voice. "I know this meeting is a little unorthodox, but I have felt for quite some time that I need to speak to you what I feel about your life, what I see in you."

I didn't know what to say, what to think. I'd never seen my dad show so much emotion.

"I've written some things down, things I believe God has shown me to be true about you." He fumbled awkwardly with the sheet of paper. "I don't know if I'm going to make it through this, so please forgive me if I have to stop."

I nodded my understanding, though my mind was bewildered. My dad had a box of Kleenex next to his chair. He was pointing at it as if to say, "I'm gonna need these!" Never in my life had I seen my dad cry. During sad movies, he always sounded like Darth Vader—breathing heavily to keep himself from breaking down.

But now, as he began to speak, he began to cry. And he wasn't the only one!

"My son, I love you." Those were his opening words— words that I had heard only one time since I was eleven, and that time had been a month earlier over the phone. Between free-flowing tears and sniffles he continued.

"I know I haven't always been there for you when you needed me, and haven't always spoken the words to you that you needed to hear. And for this, I ask your forgiveness."

And if those words weren't powerful enough, he proceeded to unload a series of statements that changed my life as a young man.

"Eric, I see you as a man. You are a mighty warrior in God's camp, a leader of His people, someone built to change this world. You will communicate to multitudes and your lips will be our lives."

If those words had been spoken by anyone other than my dad, they still would have been meaningful, but they wouldn't have changed me. But because they were my *dad's* words they made a home within my heart and now stand as beacons within my soul. My dad's words gave fuel to my manhood and fire to my confidence.

As parents, you hold an amazing verbal power in your kids' lives. You can destroy them with a single utterance or you can shape them into heroes—all with a wag of the tongue. You may be similar to my dad—his parents never spoke words of edification to him. Like him, you might find it quite daunting to open your mouth and actually speak words that will cause you to need a box of Kleenex. But, oh, how powerful those words are to your kids!

The key isn't just saying words that make your child feel good about himself, but words that help him realize the potential of his life when fully yielded to the God of the universe. When God possesses and operates a human life, there is no limit to the heavenly potential of that life.

As kids and young people, we often only see as far as our parents' words allow us to see. And often, our parents don't realize the kind of impact their words really make in our lives. We carry our parents' hurtful words into our adult years, not even realizing how they limit us and obscure the amazing potential of what God desires to do in and through our lives.

Cara was a precocious eighteen-year-old who possessed a beautiful singing voice. But though she had the talent, she refused to sing in front of an audience. She seemed socially confident and not at all reclusive, so one day I asked her why she didn't feel comfortable singing.

"When I was eight," she said, "I was singing around the house and my dad yelled out, 'Shut up, Cara! Stop singing! You can't sing!'"

Cara believed her dad, and it stunted her growth. This happens so often within home environments. The hurtful words of strangers may sting, but the hurtful words of family *cripple* us. Words like "You are an idiot!" or "You are worthless!" or "Nothing good will ever come of your life!" create massive limitations on a child's ability to allow God to use his faculties to change the world. They build superhigh walls in a child's life, hindering him from comprehending the great value God sees in him or the scope of His plans for him.

But just as hurtful words from family can devastate a young life, so honoring and encouraging words can ennoble a young life. Words like "I love you!" or "You are so precious to me!" help a child understand that she is cherished, which helps her more readily comprehend and embrace the concept of God's love. And statements such as, "God has great things in store for your life!" help young people remain open to extraordinary things rather than pitching their tent in the land of the mediocre.

This world doesn't need more self-confident kids. We need more *Christ-confident* kids—kids who realize that their body is a palace of the King of kings. We need kids who understand that great things will come when they yield to His life at work within them. We need kids who believe that if they continue down God's ancient path throughout their days on this earth, then their lives will surely be remembered with the historic heroes of old.

During my growing-up years, my dad struggled to enunciate God's thoughts to me. I was twenty-three when my dad began to speak words of heaven into my life. Though his words might have come late, they still had a life-changing impact upon my future. Even if your child is passed the early years, it is not too late to start speaking words of life to him or her. Sure, it's always better to start young, but starting today is the next best option. No matter when you take that step, it's a step that God will surely honor.

Heroic parents are those who raise Christ-confident kids— who dream God's dreams for their child's life, and then plant, at the right time, those dreams into their child's heart.

HEROIC PARENTING GOAL #4

Creating Christlike Communicators

As parents, when you deposit heaven's words into your child's life, he gains the foundation to begin pouring heaven's words into others' lives. Such words establish a pattern for children to recreate not only in their future marriages and families, but also in the world around them.

It is in the family environment that a child first begins to establish patterns for communication. And sadly, it's often in the family environment that kids learn to approach communication from a selfish vantage point rather than a selfless one. They learn that they must fight to be heard, scream for their rights, defend their behavior, and justify the way they are.

Yet, that isn't how God intended it to be. It was God's intent that family be a place where selfless communication thrives; a place where a young child feels known, understood, and listened to. Family is supposed to be an environment in which a young person feels so appreciated and loved that he or she is able to look around at the needs of others in the family and help them feel appreciated and loved too.

Most of us don't have a model for this kind of family dynamic. It appeals to us, but it sounds totally foreign. When I was growing up, it was foreign to my family too. But through a series of God-directed events within our home we slowly began to become a listening home—a family that sought to hear each other rather than just be heard.

And it was my *parents* who led the way in making that significant change. In fact, I remember vividly one of the first major moments in the transition process. I was all grown up and quite settled in my ways when it happened. My mom and I were sitting together on a screened-in porch when she suddenly looked at me and asked, "Eric, is there something that I did when you were little that is still hurting you today?"

It was a strange question. My mom was famous for asking questions, but she had never asked one quite like that.

"No," I responded with a manly grunt. "I think I've moved past my childhood just fine."

"Did it ever hurt you that I gave so much of my time ministering to other people," she went on, "and you felt that I should have given more time to you?"

Bingo! She hit something square on the head. While I was growing up, her ministry to down-and-outers had always bothered me. As a child, I had always resented the people that stole my mom from me—people with needs that seemed to absorb all her time and attention. But those things were in the past. I was a grown man now.

"That was a long time ago!" I chuckled carelessly. "Those things don't bother me anymore."

"Eric," my mom said softly, "I want you to know that I'm sorry for being insensitive in that area. I never wanted you to feel like a secondary priority in my life."

I felt some emotion rise up within my chest, but I quickly shrugged my shoulders and tried to act like this whole conversation was unnecessary.

"Eric," my mom said solemnly, "would you please come sit on my lap?"

I looked at her with a sardonic smile that said, *You've got to be kidding!* "Uh, no thanks!" I said politely.

"Eric, please," my mom persisted. "Please come and sit on your mother's lap."

I looked around for *Candid Camera* and again said, "No, I'm fine right here where I'm sitting, thank you."

It was then that my mom pulled her motherly trump card and demanded, "Eric, up on my lap!"

I got up from my chair and walked over toward my mom. (Being double her size, it was an awkward thing to figure out how to place myself on her lap!) She touched her hand against my head and gently brought it to her chest. "Eric," she said through her tears, "I just want you to know that I love you so much! I have always loved you! I love my big little boy so much!"

Her words released my emotions like a floodgate. I began to weep in my mother's arms. I was twenty-three years old, yet I wept in her arms as if I were a little boy again. Healing and forgiveness washed over my relationship with my mom that day, and I have never been the same since.

I felt understood, I felt appreciated, and I felt loved.

When my dad asked forgiveness for all the years he'd spent on the road traveling, away from us kids, and he spoke those unforgettable words, "I love you, Son!" I felt understood, I felt appreciated, and I felt loved.

A listening home is a safe place, an atmosphere where it's okay to be honest with your feelings and address your concerns straightforwardly. A listening home is the great practice ground for a Christlike communicator. It trains a child to listen to the needs of others and speak words that build and encourage. It equips a young person with the necessary verbal tools to express her unique feelings, thoughts, and ideas, to help her draw out the feelings, thoughts and ideas of others. It trains kids to be selfless in their communication and not self-serving. It trains them to listen to others instead of demanding to be heard.

Often, a listening home begins with reconciliation. It starts with asking for forgiveness and forgiving those who may have hurt you. A family environment that breeds kids that feel known is a family environment where wrongs have been set right. A child will never feel understood if the hurts he has felt growing up are never addressed and rectified.

My family still loves to sit around in the living room and listen to each other and better understand one another. There are still times when we must start this process with reconciliation and forgiveness. But this always moves into the richness of making each other feel understood, appreciated, and loved. And when we leave each other's presence, we all want to make everyone else we meet feel the same way we feel when we are part of our listening home.

When Leslie and I started our marriage, we established a listening home. The depth of emotional maturity that it brings into our lives has been amazing.

As parents, your children need to feel understood, appreciated, and loved. So build your family environment into the kind of home that loves to listen rather than just be heard. Teach your kids the amazing power of a listening home, and they'll take the lessons they learn from your example and share them with the entire world.

❖

As a parent, you don't want your child to have just a great love story, but also a great *life* story. You want him or her to make an impact on this world and truly live a heroic existence. And the secret key to all these things is simply God Himself. When God takes over a life and possesses it, He transforms it into a picture of His grace and beauty. He inspires it toward an extraordinary existence with Him at the helm. He trains it to cultivate heavenly relationships. He imbues it with a divine confidence. And He equips it with all the necessary tools to communicate His truth to this dying world.

God is in the business of building superheroic lives. He is simply asking you, as a loving parent, to join Him in the family business.

NOTES

Unhappily Ever After

1. Michelle Buford, quoted on *Oprah,* "The Secret Sex Lives of Teens" original air date 10-02-03. Copyright 2003. Harpo Productions, Inc.
2. Lisa Collier Cool, "The Secret Sex Lives of Kids," *Ladies' Home Journal* (March 2001): 56–1590. (www.lhj.com)
3. Benoit Denizet-Lewis, "Teenage Sex," *New York Times Magazine,* (May 30, 2004):30–35.

Chapter 1

1. Richard Lattimore, *Homer's Odyssey* (New York: Harper and Row Publishers, Inc., 1950), 189–90.
2. *Facts on File Encyclopedia of World Mythology and Legend,* s.v. "Orpheus."

Chapter 2

1. Adoniram Judson quoted in Edith Deen, *Great Women of the Christian Faith* (Westwood, NJ: Barbour and Company, Inc., 1959), 172.

Chapter 3
1. V. Raymond Edman, *They Found the Secret* (Grand Rapids, MI: Baker Book House, 1978), 121–26.
2. Charles Turnbull quoted in Edman, *They Found the Secret,* 120.
3. Elisabeth Elliot, *Passion and Purity* (Tarrytown, NY: Fleming H. Revell Company).
4. Elisabeth Elliot, *Shadow of the Almighty: The Life and Testament of Jim Elliot,* (San Francisco: HarperCollins, 1979), 15.

Chapter 4
1. George Barna quoted in Chuck Colson, "Any Old World View Will Do," *Perspective* (May, 1998).
2. The Voice of the Martyrs, *Hearts of Fire,* (Nashville: W Publishing Group, 2003).

Chapter 5
1. George Barna, *Third Millennium Teens* (Ventura, CA: Barna Research, 2000), 56–57.
2. The Barna Update, *The Year's Most Intriguing Findings from Barna Research Studies,* December 17, 2001. (www.barna.org)

Epilogue
1. Elisabeth Elliot, *A Chance to Die* (Grand Rapids, MI: Fleming H. Revell, 1987), 31.
2. Bishop Bardsley quoted in Amy Carmichal, *Gold Cord* (London: Society for Promoting Christian Knowledge, 1947), 159–62.
3. Edith Dean, *Great Women of the Christian Faith* (Westwood, NJ: Barbour and Company, Inc., 1959), 218–26.
4. Ibid, 141–48.
5. John G. Paton, *Missionary Patriarch—The True Story of John G. Paton* (San Antonio, TX: The Vision Forum, Inc., 2001) 17–26.
6. Elliot, *Passion and Purity,* 43.

For more information
about the ministry of Eric and Leslie Ludy,
please visit
www.whengodwrites.com